Coming Close

Coming Close

Forty Essays on Philip Levine

EDITED BY MARI L'ESPERANCE
AND TOMÁS Q. MORÍN

Prairie Lights Books, Iowa City
Distributed by the University of Iowa Press

Prairie Lights Books, Iowa City 52240
Copyright © 2013 by Prairie Lights Books
Printed in the United States of America

Design by Ashley Muehlbauer

Printed on acid-free paper
Paperback ISBNS: 978-0-9859325-2-7, 0-9859325-2-X
E-book ISBNS: 978-0-9859325-3-4, 0-9859325-3-8
LCCN: 2012949024

For my grandparents, my first teachers.
—TOMÁS Q. MORÍN

For my teachers and mentors, and for my family.
—MARI L'ESPERANCE

Mine Own Phil Levine

after W. S. Merwin

What he told me, I will tell you
There was a war on
It seemed we had lived through
Too many to name, to number

There was no arrogance about him
No vanity, only the strong backs
Of his words pressed against
The tonnage of a page

His suggestion to me was that hard work
Was the order of each day
When I asked again, he said it again,
Pointing it out twice

His Muse, if he had one, was a window
Filled with a brick wall, the left hand corner
Of his mind, a hand lined with grease
And sweat: literal things

Before I knew him, I was unknown
I drank deeply from his knowledge
A cup he gave me again and again
Filled with water, clear river water

He was never old, and never grew older
Though the days passed and the poems
Marched forth and they were his words
Only, no other words were needed

He advised me to wait, to hold true
To my vision, to speak in my own voice
To say the thing straight out
There was the whole day about him

The greatest thing, he said, was presence
To be yourself in your own time, to stand up
That poetry was precision, raw precision
Truth and compassion: genius

I had hardly begun. I asked, How did you begin
He said, I began in a tree, in Lucerne
In a machine shop, in an open field
Start anywhere

He said If you don't write, it won't
Get written. No tricks. No magic
About it. He gave me his gold pen
He said What's mine is yours

—DORIANNE LAUX

Contents

Preface

It is a mystery how projects like this one come into the world: something unnamable transpires in the confluence of inspiration, conscious intention, and opportunity—some might call it synchronicity—and the project is off and running. This anthology came to life like a spark set down in a field of September wheat—it took off quickly and grew with a furious momentum, fueled by our shared love for and gratitude to Phil for all that he has meant, and continues to mean, to us. From the time we first discussed the idea in late November 2011 to the arrival of the last essay six months later, we have continually marveled at the speed and relative ease by which this collection has come together. It is as if the stars had already formed the template and we had only to enter it. The time was ripe for a tribute to Phil, a major American poet who has given more than fifty years of his life and career to supporting and nurturing younger poets while also publishing eighteen poetry collections of his own (alongside collections of essays and translations) and winning every notable literary prize under the sun. Above all, this book has been a true labor of love for us—a gift to Phil, to all those whom he and his poems have touched, and to everyone who believes that art and a dedicated teacher can transform lives.

—MARI L'ESPERANCE AND TOMÁS Q. MORÍN

Acknowledgments

We are immensely grateful to all the poets who contributed their voices and personal relationships with Phil to this shared effort. If time and space allowed, we would have included many more, as Phil has taught and mentored countless poets over the years, far more than our anthology could accommodate. We also acknowledge Phil's students and mentees who have passed on, but who are included here in spirit. We are indebted to Jane Mead and Jan Weissmiller of Prairie Lights for choosing *Coming Close* as a debut publication of their new Prairie Lights Books, to be distributed by the University of Iowa Press. Our gratitude to Jim McCoy and everyone at the press for their dedicated work on this collection. We thank our partners, families, colleagues, and friends—too many to name here—for their support and understanding while we labored over the manuscript. Of course, these essays would not exist without Phil and his investment and belief in us, as poets and humans, and to him our gratitude is boundless.

"The Poem Circling Hamtramck, Michigan, All Night in Search of You," from *New Selected Poems* by Philip Levine, copyright © 1984, 1991 by Philip Levine, is used by permission of Alfred A. Knopf, a division of Random House, Inc.

"Mine Own Phil Levine," from *The Book of Men* by Dorianne Laux, copyright © 2011 by Dorianne Laux, is used by permission of W. W. Norton & Company, Inc.

Introduction

Their Invisible Great Good Luck

JANE MEAD

One of the great privileges of teaching, of having students, is the way it puts you in people's lives just as they are open to learning, and perhaps even open to how that learning might change them. Teaching the writing of poetry, as Philip Levine has done for decades, is a particularly intense version of this student/ teacher connection, since in many ways our poems reflect our most basic relationship to ourselves and the world around us. Writing poetry requires us to persevere through layers of half-said half-truths, reaching for that moment when we have got something true said right. It demands of us vulnerability, honesty, and devotion to craft, and in return it can give us our lives.

You might change someone's life (read *for the better*) through a chance encounter as you walk to the corner store for bread. If you choose to teach the writing of poetry, however, you increase your chances of experiencing this privilege. But even within this category of poet-teacher, when it comes to changing lives, Philip Levine, by all accounts, has surpassed all probability. Gathered here are a handful of essays that speak of his (not always immediately appreciated) honesty, his commitment to poetry and to his students, his humor, and his generosity. These essays are love letters—thank-you notes for some of the great gifts. These former students understand what Larry Levis calls "the invisible great good luck" of having had Phil as a teacher.

You don't have to know Phil very long—thirty seconds or so will do—to see that he's got one of the world's most fine-tuned shit detectors, and his reputation as a *brutal* (et cetera) teacher seems to have been legendary: many of his former students here write about the terror they felt anticipating their first encounter with the monster. But this "brutality" became the quality those students most cherished as they rose to the occasion of his frank and direct responses to their poems. Leaving aside the question of what the *rarity* of that directness might suggest about our culture in general, or about the MFA culture in particular, those students who came to value Phil's criticism of their poems did so because they understood that he was saving them a great deal of time, and that this was so because "he was right," as they often seem to have sensed immediately. In other words, Phil was speaking to something they already knew, nourishing something essential within them that their worlds and selves did not know how to value. He was giving them a tuning fork. "Philip Levine gifted me a way to my life," writes Shane Book, and "to have been a student in Levine's classes . . . was to have [my life] *given* to me by another," writes Larry Levis, who recommended Phil's class to David St. John, who recommended Phil's class to Mike Clifton, etc.

As his students became aware of Phil's regard for poetry—"it's the most important thing you will ever do in your life"—his famous disdain for anything that didn't ring true, or for simply bad poetry, contributed to their understanding that poetry was just too important to play around with. That he was hard on them meant he took poetry *and their poems* seriously: they learned to take themselves and their poetry seriously—because Phil did. Poetry, a sense of being fully alive, speaking fully to one another: these are big life-altering gifts, gifts so fully human that the distinction between giver and receiver breaks down. In some essential way, his students became aware, too, that the teaching/learning of poetry writing was both the catalyst and the gold. How you wrote was a reflection of how you lived, and there was no time to pussyfoot around. You might enter his workshop (as did Xochiquetzal Candelaria) thinking, "Oh, shit! No one is going to understand my work unless I pretend I'm someone else," but you would leave knowing that nobody would believe or care about your work (including yourself) unless you learned how to speak as yourself. Phil was direct and blunt, but he was not cruel; many of the students here speak of his caring, his careful listening, his instinctive understanding when a student had had all he or she could take in. They laughed a lot, too, and drank a little red wine now and again; that was important—that was part of being alive together.

As it does for so many of those readers unknown to him, the subject matter of Phil's poems legitimized the lives of his students in other ways. Joseph O. Legaspi's sentiments are echoed again and again when he says, "Philip gave me license to write about the people in my life: working-class immigrants whose tiniest of lives were no less valid, complicated, and sacred." In this way, Phil's students "not only found a way to speak, but were reassured of their right to" (Kathy Fagan). Conversely, Phil's poems "startled me awake from my middle-class point of view," writes Sharon Olds, and "prepared me to be more ready to see my (woman's) life as worthy of song." What could be more important than these relationships, to our selves and our worlds? What could be more inherently political? David St. John sums it up beautifully: "Phil was also a model to us all . . . His presence was fiercely political in the most human way; that is, he reminded us that poetry creates empathy for those marginalized by their societies, and that to live responsibly and to write with conscience were crucial elements of being a poet."

Literal-minded as I am, I declined to write an essay for this book because I was never Phil's student. Or was I? Wasn't it that book of his with the red cover (*Seven Years from Somewhere*, I now think) that I tucked under my arm when I walked out to the beach near Port Townsend, Washington, where, BA in economics in hand, I had fled the East Coast to work for the Forest Service? Deciding to educate myself in contemporary poetry, I had somehow come to Phil's book, to his poems, just at the moment when the slight nudge might push me to embrace once again the thinking-music that had absorbed me as a child-writer of child-poems. I read something there (I no longer remember what) that made me decide to do this thing—to learn to say what I knew. Before I tucked the book under my arm, I checked the name of the author again. Surely the Port Townsend library, home to my favorite cookbook, *LO, the Mighty Potato*, would have more books by Philip Levine?

Many of the essays in this book speak to such moments, such tipping points, followed by a trek to Fresno or New York, Boston or Houston to study with this man who seemed to many, particularly his working-class students, to open a world of possibility, a man who managed to push a good number of the next generation or two of poets to honor themselves and their worlds, by teaching them to honor their poems. We have a smattering of Phil's students represented here. What of all the others? And what of *their* students? And those influenced by his poems and subject matter who have never met him? And what about all those for whom his letters were a lifeline? We'll never know the whole of it; we never do.

What I *do* know is that Phil consistently shows immeasurable kindness, as well as generosity of time and spirit, to a remarkable number of writers, including myself, who was never even his formal student. Subsequent to his choosing my first book for publication, I met Phil and his wife, Franny, and later visited them in New York and Fresno, where the love and respect they quietly showed for one another, the ease and humor of their households, was remarkable—as noted by many of the essayists represented here. I was most struck by their sheer *sanity*. Had Phil had other talents or settled into other jobs, surely he would have touched lives. It is our good fortune, however, that he came to poetry and to teaching—and in so doing touched *so many* lives. Thank you, Phil, from us all.

Coming Close

A Laureate in Letters

Philip Levine in Correspondence, 1994–2011

AARON BELZ

Philip Levine and I have exchanged almost 150 letters over the past seventeen years. I met him while pursuing a master's in creative writing at New York University. He was the only professor there with the courage to publicly shred his students' poems—shredded some of mine into oblivion, as I recall. "Not one of these lines means anything," he would say, or, "Most of what happens to you in a day is not worth writing about." But he was also, at least in my case, the most affirming of teachers: "Looks like we have a young Hart Crane here," he once said after reading one of my poems, and so I zealously read *The Bridge* to figure out what he meant. Turned out he was wrong. He was wrong a lot, and not afraid to admit it.

I first wrote to him in 1994 when I'd heard from a friend at Duke University's short-lived *DoubleTake Magazine* that Levine had agreed to write an essay on the closing of my in-laws' White Furniture Company. For more than a century, White had been the heart of the Mayberryesque town of Mebane, North Carolina—now little more than an exurb for nearby Chapel Hill and Burlington. Levine, with his reputation for documenting working-class America, was a logical choice for this assignment. I was delighted at the connection, of course, and exploited it. I now realize that there didn't need to be an occasion for a letter to Levine—or Phil, of "Yours, Phil," as I and many others have come to think of him.

In August of 2011, when headlines began to appear saying that Levine had been appointed United States Poet Laureate, I wasn't surprised. Having already claimed a Pulitzer, a National Book Award, a National Book Critics Circle Award, a Ruth Lilly Poetry Prize, and many other laurels, and representing, as he is said to, the voice of the American heartland, he seemed a natural choice for poetry's highest office. For his part, he claimed to be "stunned" (*Los Angeles Times*, August 12, 2011), a characteristic response and not at all false humility. Levine is an authentic skeptic, one who sees good things as bonuses and doesn't take himself or other people too seriously. Failures and successes are to be expected in equal measure along the way.

In evidence, and with the author's permission, here are several excerpts from his letters to me. I'll avoid the newsy or personal remarks, the cranky asides (of which there are plenty), and comments on my own poems. Instead, I'll sample the wisdom—advice for a clueless young writer, straight from the pen of a successful postwar-era, post-Romantic atheistic humanist, someone who'd clearly had it with the "bizniz" of American poetry but still believed in America, or at least the basic idea of America, and very much believed in poetry.

I'll begin with the passage that was and still is most helpful to me. I've not only used it as a benchmark in my own career, but have quoted parts of it to my creative writing students and young poets who e-mail me asking for advice. The key word is *doggedness*:

> You asked for detailed advice on how to deal with taking yourself seriously as a poet & yet not puffing yourself up & at the same time believing in yourself as a poet. I can tell you this: long before I believed in what I was writing I believed in myself as a poet, believed I had something to say but had not yet found out how to say it. I suppose I was saying to myself, Philip, you are a person of intelligence, feelings, wit, some charm, you have as much right to this poetry thing as anyone else, though it is obvious that some others are more gifted (Hart Crane, John Keats, Wilfred Owen, etc., I was not yet 25), so stick at this thing & see what happens. No harm will come from this doggedness. I don't recall if I actually said just that, but I know I thought just that. I know also that I love imaginative writing & that it had meant something magical to me, & I believed I could add my pennyweight to it. And I have.

My sense of humor certainly helped. Not a day passed during which I did not laugh at myself: "The very thought, Levine as poet! Ha ha!" (November 30, 1995)

In the same letter, Levine has this to say about getting poems out there: "Don't worry about not publishing yet. Most of the poets I know who published early got big heads & perished as poets. Or became obsessed with the bizniz of poetry & became that sort of jerk bizniz poet. A few saw through that shit & came back to poetry, but most became sad fools. Send the poems to any magazine you like & see what happens; it won't do any harm."

I've followed both hemispheres of this advice and have had success in doing so. Although I'm not a great poet, I'm good enough to compete with what's out there (most of which is also not great), and I'm especially good when I truly don't care what editors think about me. It frees me from all prejudice, lets me do my personal thing (which is nerdy and weird), and encourages me to do so "doggedly." Leave it up to editors to make the call. I earned independence from Levine. Much more recently, I also learned from him the inner workings of the writing process:

[You must] find a way to let the "other" fellow speak in your poems. He might embarrass you at first . . . When the noise fades & you welcome the silence, that other heretofore silent fellow will speak IF you are listening. Don't rush it; just let the game come to you, as they say in tennis. Now for a vision, you must go back into the earlier you, the one who lived a life with a vision, but don't take that vision, that was then, you were a lad with a lad's vision; don't throw it away. No, no, you must honor it. Let it be the rich compost in which the present vision will grow. Then you can leave it where it is. (July 17, 2009)

When I quoted this back to him saying I would "keep this advice," he wrote back cringing—in a letter now apparently lost. He commented that he couldn't believe he'd written those words or that I would think them worth keeping.

A final aspect of Levine's letters I've found instructive is his forays into transcendent questions. Although his preferred range is the tangible (such as jazz and baseball), he addresses the question of God from time to time. And although he styles himself an atheist, he allows for the possibility of God's existence, seems even deistic in some passages. I broached the subject once when working on a review of Mark Jarman's *Questions for Ecclesiastes*, which

3

I interpreted as putting God in the dock, and Levine had this to say: "Frankly I don't blame God for anything, not even the fact I'm getting old. He/she got no time to worry about me, he's got to see that the tides behave. There's a lot that's wrong with the world, but most of it seems the work of people. Greed, racism, the inequalities of opportunity, the cold closed hearts that abound—all of that's our doing" (December 12, 1996).

I have come to agree deeply with this view of human responsibility, born for Levine of hard twentieth-century experience (and which he underscores in a later letter by saying, "It wasn't God who urged Christians to slaughter Jews, for centuries"). Whatever God might represent to Levine, he/she is not a mere projection of the imagination: "The other day (night) in class I responded to a poem which declared, 'God is a feeling . . . ' I responded with some heat & surprised the class by taking exception to the claim. I could almost hear their thoughts: 'This atheist Jew is claiming God exists outside our own collective emotions! He's lost his mind'" (October 25, 1995).

For Levine, and now also for me, this sense of responsibility finally resolves in poetry, even if the work we do—both the art we make and the desire to make it—has a tendency to slip our grasp. He concluded one letter memorably: "I'm now trying to get back to poetry one more time. I seem to do this over & over. There's no end to it. There's nothing to stop me now except myself. Perhaps the same is true for you. So let's get on with it. Tennis on, but I'm not watching. They can go on without me" (August 30, 1997).

This spring, on the way to give a reading in Davis, California, I had an opportunity to visit Phil and his wife, Franny, at their modest home in Fresno. Franny prepared boeuf bourguignon and poured wine. They introduced me to the fruit trees in their massive backyard. We ate together and ended the evening with a glass of scotch and some talk of New York University. Finally they put me up at a nearby hotel. I've never experienced a more welcoming stop on the weary, low-paying road of poetry. I hope that my own road comes to a similar end.

There's more worth saying and remembering from my correspondence with Philip Levine, but I suppose it will have to wait—in his own words—until somebody cares to peruse it in a "yellowing archive." Meanwhile, there's the poetry.

Rhymes with Deer

CIARAN BERRY

We were about three poems into the semester, and I wanted to see what the great man had written on my latest effort. I thought his words would provide me with some insight, tell me something I needed to know as an apprentice poet, and as someone more or less new to the concept of workshops. I was in need of a guru, a hairy shaman who would point me down the absolute path to poetic certainty. This was in the graduate Creative Writing Program at New York University, which at the time was still housed at 19 University Place just off Washington Square Park. We met around an oval table in the student lounge on Wednesday evenings. I sat to Phil's left, beside Ryan Black and directly across the table from Sarah Heller. I'd been in the country about four years, and much about the United States was still strange to me.

My undergraduate experience of the creative writing workshop had involved a single class with the young Northern Irish novelist Robert McLiam Wilson at the University of Ulster. We sat in Robert's office in a cloud of cigarette smoke talking about our god-awful poems and stories; or cricket, or politics, or our teacher's handsomeness (he looked like a literary Pierce Brosnan, he said so himself). Once, he wrote "DE HEANEY IT!" in red pen across a poem of mine that involved someone drowning in a peat bog. He also suggested that, as an exercise, we write about either giving or receiving fellatio. Much later, having moved to New York City with my new wife, I took a couple of classes at the 92nd Street Y. These were mostly full of retired doctors and lawyers who assumed that their successful professional lives assured their success in poetry, which of course turned out not to be the case.

So this was a relatively new thing then—my first workshop as a poetry student at NYU with the reputably fierce and fickle, not to mention wickedly funny, Phil Levine. True to his reputation, he'd upset a couple of girls on the first night we gathered. One was writing poems in the voices of buried-alive Victorians; the other believed that punctuation was just a convention. So, too, is language, Phil pointed out.

In that first discussion, he kept my poem for last. I assumed, therefore, that it was terrible, but he was reasonably kind when it finally rose to the top of the pile. My poem was more American than the poems of all the Americans in the class, he said. Parts of it reminded him of Whitman, parts of it of Crane. I took the train back to Queens knowing I needed to reread both poets, just as I often left Phil's class thinking about what I hadn't read well enough or at all. Dylan Thomas. Edward Thomas. Antonio Machado. Wallace Stevens. Miguel Hernández. Galway Kinnell, who Phil always said was the greatest poet of their generation.

But we were three weeks into the class now, and I really wanted to know what more deeply, if anything, he thought of my work. I was still too chicken to go to office hours. Even though he wasn't in our workshop, Adam Day from Louisville had practically moved into Phil's office by then. You'd walk past and there Adam would be, feet stretched out, hands cupped behind his head, like Phil was his bookie or favorite uncle, as they went through a poem or talked about Larry Levis, Phil's former student, and the poet, along with Phil himself, whom most of us wanted to be. I envied Adam his ease; I was still too much in awe. I'd tiptoe past the door hoping the maestro wouldn't notice me and call me in: "Hey, it's our Irish guy. Irish guy, have you met Kentucky?"

Halfway through our three-hour weekly session, we'd take a little break. Phil would saunter down to the bathroom in his white tennis shoes. Star student Matt Donovan would slip down to the street to buy a quick bit of supper. Usually, he brought back a slice of pizza, which he was adept at folding in two so he could eat and walk at the same time in that way one masters only after many years in New York City. One night he brought back sushi. Phil

6

just couldn't resist. He leaned over and pointed at Matt's dinner. "You like that shit?" he asked me with more than a little glee.

We laughed, of course, as we did so much in Phil's presence—when he told us of his escapades with John Berryman, or how Robert Lowell had little time for Phil's poetry but had once helped him buy a pair of new glasses, or any of the countless anecdotes he shared about several renowned literary figures in a way that a more politic poet never would have dared. Tears and laughter together, Phil's workshop was a bit like an Irish wedding or wake. I loved his honesty, the sense that just because someone had a big name and a book contract with a major publishing house didn't mean he or she automatically had our teacher's respect. His stories helped to make us feel like we were coconspirators in our patchy poetic practice rather than pilgrims come to pay homage at his table. In fact, Phil had no time for those students who came to worship. He could smell the muskrat from a mile off.

After the workshop, the stories continued when I did finally pluck up the courage to visit Phil during office hours, when I'd show up at his readings, or when he and Fran met me, Colin Cheney, and Lorraine Doran (two other former students, though from different years) for dinner in Brooklyn Heights. For a poet of his stature, Phil has always been remarkably generous with his time. He's that rare thing: a major poet who actually loves to teach, and who hasn't been driven half crazy by his needy students. He answers our e-mails. He writes letters to us. He cares about what's going on in our lives—the ones that involve writing, and the ones that involve wives, husbands, children, dogs, cats, and usually dreary work.

The last time I benefited from Phil's generosity, and the last time I saw him and Fran, was at the Aldeburgh Poetry Festival in Suffolk, England, in 2009. I was there as the absolute bottom-of-the-bill poet, the winner of the festival's first book competition, whereas Phil was of course the star, that year's all-American poetic champion, the face on the front of the brochure. Somehow, though, there I was at his dinner table, in his swanky seafront hotel, smiling gleefully as all the other poets looked on and no doubt wondered, why him, why not me? What could that obscure Irishman possibly have to say to the great Phil Levine when I could be in his seat?

I can't remember what we talked about that night. The wine, the sausages Phil was enjoying, news of other students who'd been in that workshop at NYU whom Phil remembered and always asked after; Berryman and Lowell; how Geoffrey Hill, who'd read earlier in the day, reminded me of Dumbledore

7

from the Harry Potter books; horse racing, jazz, Irish whisky; the English weather; my new job and whether it was less dreary than my previous one; my wife and son; why no one would accept the paper pound note Phil had held over from his last trip to England twenty or so years before, the entire British economy having long since switched to the pound coin.

We must have talked about all of this and more. We drank. Phil, modest as ever about his own work, told me not to bother coming to his reading the next day. I'd heard him too often before, he said, and it would be "the same old shit." It's worth mentioning that the entire audience stood up and clapped hard after that reading, until long after he'd left the stage. Every moment I spent in Phil's presence that weekend was a gift. I was watching not just a great poet in his natural element, but a great ambassador for poetry—American, Spanish, English, even Welsh.

Of all the meager gifts we receive as poets, I think the deep friendships, the sense of kinship born of a common endeavor, are perhaps the richest, the most rewarding. If we were to rely on book sales (though I'm sure Phil has sold plenty), or fan letters, or the pride of our increasingly silent and suspicious families, or the imaginary groupies hanging around after our readings to sustain us, we'd be well and truly disappointed. It's worth raising a glass of Jameson or Bushmills to the fact that Phil, to so many of us—and most especially to his students, before most of us were published, before we could even conjure a half-competent line or afford to pay for our own meals—has been a friend and an ally as well as a teacher.

Whenever I see old friends from NYU, whether they were in that first workshop or not, the conversation about our time in the program almost always circles back to Phil. With Anthony Carelli, I still talk about him. With Ryan Black and Matt Donovan. With Kathy Graber, who never actually took Phil's class. With Brian McDonald. Our former teacher's ears must burn often with our talk and our laughter. Ten years later, we're still thinking of the things he told us about our work, how he praised us when praise was due but never let us believe in our own bullshit. We're still reading the poets whose names we heard breathed out into that room around that oval table. Zbigniew Herbert. James Wright. William Carlos Williams. John Keats. Cesare Pavese. Miguel Hernández. César Vallejo.

Throughout that first semester, Phil didn't know quite what to do with my first name. In this he had much in common with the rest of the United

States. Ciaran just doesn't look like it could ever be pronounced the way it is. On the phone, telemarketers still try it out as *See Aran* or *Clarin*, as if I were an advert for those famous islands off the coast of County Galway or a new allergy medicine. Occasionally they'll even ask for *Sharon*, which makes it all the easier to hang up. Even when I pronounce my name, people struggle. They hear *Kiernan*, which is a surname rather than a first name, or something close to *Key Ring*. "Remind me again how to say your name," Phil would say before he talked about my poems. "Say it again, louder this time."

The room at 19 University Place momentarily empty, I moved over to my teacher's pile of papers and looked down at what he'd written on my third offering. Alas, I did not find there the words that would assure my poetic destiny, or even fix that week's feeble effort. Though I often still find myself picking over the wisdom of things Phil told me, I'm also reminded of the fact that he was an incredibly modest teacher. He didn't claim to like everything, nor did he claim he could fix everything.

In blue pen, in a single sentence alongside the flabby lines of a poem I'd later abandon, he had written just a little note to self on the pronunciation of my moniker. *Ciar-an—Rhymes with Deer* was all that was there for me to contemplate.

I returned to my seat and awaited the regathering of the class, the continuation of the night's discussion.

Philip Levine, Professional Wrestling, and Me

PAULA BOHINCE

I arrived in New York City in September 1999. I was twenty-three, set to begin the MFA program at New York University, and working full time as a secretary at the university to receive tuition remission and make rent on a tiny, shared studio. The enormousness and pace of the city, the very idea of being at NYU, were enlivening and overwhelming. The death of my father two years earlier had gutted me, and, in the hectic atmosphere of the city, in its newness, I felt for the first time that I was able to catch my breath from grieving. I felt ready for something wonderful. I was poised to step into my first graduate workshop, led by Philip Levine.

I'd been warned by a few second-year students that Phil was tough. I was too shy to ask, "How tough?" or what that might even mean. I went to the first meetings nearly trembling. To my enormous relief, he seemed to like my poems. When he was tough, it felt honest and entirely generous. It would have been much easier, as a teacher, for him to glide along, skimming and praising, never really engaging. But he wanted to see us develop, caring enough to push us as we would have to push ourselves when our program ended.

In the classroom, Phil was completely present, funny, and charming. I'd been writing about heavy subjects (poverty, death, Depression-era Appalachia), and one week I decided to take a radical break on one poem: a trying-to-be-funny *ars poetica* wherein the poem was an alley and the poet a burglar, or some other terrible extended metaphor. I held my breath for Phil's reaction because I still so strongly wanted his approval. I think the summary of his critique was the exclamation, "It's a rat-fuck poem!" He said this with such delighted surprise, with such a canny grin, that I was relieved and equally delighted. I could play and deviate, and Phil would still like *me*. It was exactly what I needed. (And that fantastic phrase, naturally, has stuck with me during the years since.)

I felt like the whole world of poetry was in that room: the range of it reflected by Phil's friendship with us. He'd say something about Keats or Dickinson and then finish with, "but *they* were geniuses." Always uttered with a joyfully wry smile, as if to say, "Tough luck for us then!," including himself. *Always* including himself. That was another quality that made Phil such an incredible teacher. He let us into the struggle to create, teaching us that mastery was impossible, but to keep striving nevertheless. Be serious about the work, but remember the *joy* in it, and from it.

I still can see him at the head of the table, leaning back in his chair, his fingers laced behind his head, and then suddenly leaning forward, hands tensed on the desk, his whole body passionately engaged in his point. He *talked* to us; we didn't just move from student poem to student poem without looking up. What a *relief* to look up, to breathe, to think about larger questions in poetry, and to delight in them. Phil didn't seem tortured or troubled by poetry, or put upon by teaching. He was excited to be with us, and it showed, and it created for us an atmosphere of rigorous pleasure.

Soon after our semester began, I stopped by during one of his office hours. I asked him about "They Feed They Lion," a poem that I love deeply. Every time I encounter it on the page, without fail, I have the same reaction: when I reach the line "From 'Bow Down' come 'Rise Up'" my eyes fill with tears. The voice in that poem feels like the voice of God, and I can't help but think about my own people: in work and in poverty. We talked about Detroit and the dialect in that line. I said how the stanzas, to me, seemed to shift in the manner of a gear shift; I had no better language to describe what I felt was happening. He was so forgiving of my inarticulateness, so lovely, and said that yes, he'd wanted the poem to gain a kind of momentum in that way.

Later that same meeting, I mentioned professional wrestling, I think because I'd made a reference to one of the old-timers (Bobo Brazil or Buddy Rogers) in one of my poems. My father had loved pro wrestling, and so I had also, as a young girl. Phil, quite surprisingly, told me that when his mother was in her nineties she'd been wild for it. I felt such warmth and camaraderie suddenly. I liked thinking of his elderly mother getting riled up at the dramatics and action, shouting at the TV, the same way my dad had, and I had. Most of all, I felt grateful that, upon my sharing something about my father, Phil met it in such a generous way.

After that semester, I saw Phil maybe two more times at readings, there with his beautiful wife, Franny. We've kept in touch by letters in the decade since. Every time I get one from him, it's still so moving. I look at the spidery, slanting, masculine handwriting on the envelope and don't want to open it yet. I let it sit on my desk for a while and then open carefully and savor it.

We began corresponding in one of my most difficult times: just after the events of September 11, 2001. I was afraid in all kinds of ways, newly graduated with an MFA, living in Queens, with no publications, cobbling together several part-time jobs, reading and writing in every spare moment. I felt put out, laid low. I'd gone from feeling that I had a place at NYU, with a purpose and schedule and colleagues, to the sudden loneliness and (literal) terror of the afterward. To begin to try to climb out, toward anything, toward *poetry*, felt impossible, and harrowing.

His letters—he must have known how I was feeling and the connection that I needed—felt, and continue to feel, miraculous to me. From time to time, I'd include a poem, and he was always encouraging. I've wanted, all of these years, to make him proud and to feel worthy of the time he spent on me. From his poems, which sustain me, to the care he took of us in the workshop, to his kindness to me in the years beyond: gifts beyond measure.

When I think of Phil Levine, my teacher and friend, I always go back to that moment in his office, talking about his mother and my father, what they had instead of poetry, our love for them shining, and the poetry that makes the expression of that love possible.

Mine Own Philip Levine

SHANE BOOK

One ridiculously hot September I arrived at New York University not knowing what Philip Levine, who was to be my teacher that fall, looked like. I had seen only an old author photograph of him, possibly from the 1970s, in which he wears a tracksuit and necklace. Young and strong, with his thick, dark hair and mustache, he looks like a soccer coach. I could say I accepted the school's admission offer because I wanted to live in Manhattan or because the school gave me a scholarship, but the real reason was they had Philip Levine.

It was the first day of school and the English Department had arranged a cocktail party for graduate students to meet one another. Perhaps because of nerves, we first-year students took it upon ourselves to steer the event toward bacchanalia. There were, after all, sweaty cold cuts, stinky cheeses, and bitter wines to be attacked—and all of it free! In no time I was quite drunk.

At some point the program director, a woman of infinite graciousness, introduced the scholarship students. We had been warned about this. It was why I arrived at the cocktail party in the only formal piece of clothing I owned: a navy blazer my mother bought for me when I graduated from high school.

The program director announced my name and people clapped. Red wine and the knowledge that this might be the only time in my life anyone would give me money to write and study poetry prompted me to stand on a chair beside the cheese table and publicly thank the program. Once up there I decided to take advantage of the crowd's full attention and make a public plea. As I uttered the words "I'm homeless, so if anyone knows a room I can rent, come talk to me," I lost my footing and fell, landing on the cheese table and rolling down its length into the arms of the program secretary, an affable southern gentleman who cradled me while I struggled to resume an upright position. Peeling smoked Gouda circles off my blue polyester blazer, I became aware that the room had gone dead quiet. "I'm fine, I'm fine," I said. In his southern drawl the program secretary whooped, "Now it's a real party!" The crowd broke out laughing. I walked off in search of more wine.

Everywhere empty bottles forested the tables. On a back corner table I spied what was surely the party's final half-full hope. I walked over and asked the older gentleman sitting close to the bottle if I could have some. "Get your own," he said. "But this is the last of it," I said. I put my hand on the bottle. He put his hand on the bottle. I asked him again. He did not relinquish his grip. We stalemated a moment until I yanked the bottle from him, slopped some of the red stuff into my plastic glass, gulped it, and stomped off.

What felt like hours—yet was probably minutes—slithered by. Someone pronounced the party over; it was time for class. I piled food on a paper plate and followed some students into an ancient squeaky elevator. Three floors up, we exited onto a barely painted white hallway maze of exposed wall pipes and water-stained ceiling tiles, stopping finally at a windowless room, the words "Poetry Workshop" handwritten on a sheet of paper taped to the doorframe.

Twelve of us sat around a large, rectangular wooden table; the teacher's seat was empty. We waited. It was the first day of school when everyone wants to make a good impression, and all I could do was concentrate on keeping my head from lolling.

A good ten minutes passed before we heard a voice from the hallway, "They always put the poets in the crappy rooms." The man I had wrestled the wine bottle away from walked slowly and carefully into the room and sat in the teacher's chair. I started sweating.

Philip Levine was much older than in his author photograph. Hair thinner and grey, he was shorter than I expected, but he still had that strong, upright bearing. His eyes scanned our faces. I stared at a water stain on the gnarly carpet, wishing to end my homelessness by disappearing into that stain for the next fourteen weeks. I looked up just as Levine's glance arrived at mine.

His face betrayed no glint of recognition. I thought, maybe he's as drunk as I am and doesn't remember me.

Levine asked whether anyone had a poem to discuss. One student raised his hand, passed out copies. Immediately I resolved to forever hate this guy who made the rest of us look like the unprepared louts we surely were, and then just as quickly I felt my head start to loll, and in trying to halt the lolling, I forgot who and what to hate.

The poet finished reading his poem; comments trickled in. People were timid, offering neutral observations, "I really love the bathroom sink image" and so on. Finally Levine turned to the student: "I know what happened here. You were writing your poem and the phone rang. It was your mother who wanted to tell you something about your crazy uncle and pretty soon an hour went by before you hung up and got back to writing the poem. But by then you'd forgotten where you were going with the poem and it wandered away from you. When writing, never pick up the phone, even if it's your mother." With a pen, Levine drew a line between the third and fourth stanzas of the six-stanza poem. "The bottom half is awful. Send the bottom half to *The New Yorker* because they publish crummy poems. I should know, they print mine all the time! But they pay money for poetry. Real money!" He smiled broadly. "Send the top half to the *Shit Creek Review*; they pay nothing, but they publish good work."

We moved on to another student who had the audacity to show up for class prepared. The student read her poem; other students lobbed softball comments in her general direction. Emboldened by Levine's example, I made a criticism, something about the poem lacking an ending. There was silence. Levine looked at me as though seeing me for the first time. And then the author of some of the first poems I'd ever loved, one of my literary heroes and the reason I had come to NYU in the first place, leaned forward and in a loud voice somehow made more authoritative by its Detroit-ish inflections said, "What are you, a fucking idiot?"

Partly because I was drunk, and possibly because his question—in tone and content—felt like something my father or grandfather might have asked, and undoubtedly because when I thought on it for a second, I knew what I'd said was at best unconsidered and at worst stupid, I laughed. And Levine laughed. And I had the feeling I'd found a mentor.

I tell this story because it holds the key to Levine's success as a teacher. He folded tough feedback into an outrageous sense of humor so that if he was calling your poem the pile of dreck it had become, you could take it because he made you laugh. You had to laugh; the alternative was to weep. Levine wanted us to know how tough it was to write well. He wanted us to know what we were in for.

He spoke of how for much of his writing life he'd been neglected, accolades coming later in his career. When he taught us, only three years had passed since, as a youthful sixty-seven-year-old, he'd won the Pulitzer Prize. Awards were not important. Knowing why you were writing was important. Listening to Levine, one began to understand that by persistence, by focusing on his writing and ignoring his detractors, he'd been able to overcome them. To make it through, Levine had to be tough. The lesson was we had to be tough, too.

Those who somehow did not know his personal history of growing up a scrappy working-class kid in Detroit, making a living as a young man in a succession of automobile assembly plants, had only to visit him during office hours to see that his toughness was genuine. There, one would find a man in white tennis shoes, jeans, and a white T-shirt that looked like he'd won it at bingo tipped back in his chair eating an entire apple, including the core.

One week I dropped by his office to find him complaining of a sore arm. I chalked it up to the routine aches of being a seventy-year-old man until he revealed he had strained it pumping iron during a regular workout with his lifting partner, the 1958 Mr. Universe. He was keeping his mind sharp and his body fit for the long game.

In this long game, Levine had his aesthetic biases and made them perfectly clear. He displayed little patience for current avant-garde writing, for example. We could take or leave his assessments, but we couldn't ignore them, which is another way of saying he gave us something to push against. If praise came less frequently, it was because our poems were mostly hopeless. I do remember him defending certain students' poems when he seemed to sense the student poet was fragile or had already been through enough at the hands of his or her peers. He did not employ a one-size-fits-all approach to student work. He read people, determining how much Levine-style honesty they could take.

Levine's honesty told us he took this thing called "poetry" seriously. Therefore, he took us seriously. He believed in the dignity of work and the value of great poetry and that writing good poetry was difficult work and therefore it was necessary to write what we really cared about. We were to try very hard and not waste each other's time.

Levine was the first to admit his own failings, his struggles to write well. Asked about dealing with writer's block, he responded: "If you're having trouble writing, lower your standards. I find it works for me." We felt he was walking with us, not above us. Once, a student defended another student's work by saying Neruda had done a similar thing in a poem. Levine replied: "Yeah, but he's Neruda. He's a fucking genius! The rest of us are just humble workers in the fields of poetry."

His interest in humble, ordinary people was reflected in his own work. In this way he reminded us that our own humble origins could be fodder for literature. He had an outsider's perspective on poetry's professionalization, lamenting that it had become an industry. During his office hours he spoke of the poetry world's pettiness: "Poets are so vicious," he said, "because the stakes are so low." Yet, if the intensity with which he scrutinized our poems was any measure, the stakes were much higher than he let on.

But this was emphatically not about writing for posterity. He told us it was useless to try to predict which authors would be read after they died. He pointed to a host of different anthologies missing certain great poets, while including reams of mediocre ones—depending on the fashions of the editors' eras. He was pessimistic about his own chances, joking he'd be lucky if anyone read him next year.

To me, Levine's longevity seems assured in two ways. First, there are the poems: passionate depictions of ordinary people—people like most of us—who would not have found themselves in poems until Philip Levine wrote about them. Levine advocates for us with rage, indignation, and an unabashed tenderness, sweetness, and respect. Second is the legacy of students he taught. For five decades, Philip Levine provided countless students with an example of how to live as artists: with honesty, integrity, curiosity, cleverness, a stubborn refusal to quit, and the ability to laugh at everyone, especially themselves.

Without him I would have dropped out of graduate school. Indeed, I decided to return for a second year only after he assured me he would be back to teach again the next fall. My poems and I needed more Levine, and all three of us knew it. After NYU I went to the Iowa Writers' Workshop—an institution he had attended, yet was skeptical of. Still, as he said: "If they're giving you money, they're giving you time to write. You could do worse." After Iowa I followed what he'd done fifty years before and attended the Stegner Fellowship program at Stanford University. I did those things because he had done them first. There were no artists or writers in my family. I was starting out, and I needed a model. As I have spent my adulthood since then immersed in art and literature, I think it is not too much to say that Philip Levine gifted me a way to my life.

Changed Utterly

B. H. BOSTON

Poetry builds the blood and transforms us. It can save lives. At least that's been my experience. I would never have had anything approaching a full life, would never have taught literature and writing or edited magazines or presumed to write poems, probably would never have survived into my sixties without Philip Levine's poetry, friendship, and tutelage over the past forty-six years.

I first heard Phil read at the Fresno Public Library during what must have been the end of my senior year of high school in 1964. I'd recently purchased *On the Edge* at Dodgson's bookstore, a godsend on Van Ness Avenue downtown that—along with Stanley's Armenian Deli on the one side and Anastasia's Tobacco Shop on the other—was paramount among my favorite haunts during my first two years in the Central Valley, a place distressingly immune to the life of the imagination. Or so it seemed to me until I met Philip Levine.

As he leaned over the lectern that afternoon, squinting his left eye at the twenty or thirty of us scattered among numerous empty chairs, he remarked that in fact he *had* read to a smaller group before, "in the back of a station wagon once." He then proceeded to read with such ferocity and wit that the molecules of the air began to pulse at a quickened rate.

A year earlier, while doing chin-ups on a mulberry branch in our Sanger backyard, I announced, in response to my mother's question regarding my future—my parents were fans of *Dr. Kildare* and envisioned me in white coat with stethoscope—that more than anything else I wanted to be a poet. (I'd been writing sonnets to Marsha, who would soon become my wife, for months.) Phil's performance that Sunday afternoon at the library pretty much sealed the deal.

The next year as a freshman at Fresno State, I met a funny guy named Gene Winder. An ex-Marine already into his thirties, Gene was also an enormously talented and somewhat eccentric student poet. We soon became close friends. A senior, Gene was student teaching Latin and translating Catullus. Most notably for our purposes here, he had already studied poetry writing with Philip Levine.

One late summer morning after meteorology class, I stopped by Gene's house with two quarts of beer to find him out near the uncovered slab of the patio, a lit cigar between his teeth, his bare belly swelling above his Bermuda shorts, and a white Stetson with a rounded crown precariously balanced on his head—one of two we'd bought at a West Side used-hat shop, in lieu of actual bowlers, in homage to *Waiting for Godot*.

Apparently, Gene had donned his writing hat that day to set his entire overgrown backyard on fire—he refused to plant or mow a lawn—and stood up to his waist in weeds, garden hose in hand, surrounded by thick umber smoke and flames, attempting some semblance of control by dousing the fence line and dampening the edges of the conflagration as it advanced toward his oxfords.

"Hey, Buddy-buddy!" he shouted. "Time for Andy Griffith yet?"

Along with our devotion to Samuel Beckett, William Carlos Williams, and Dylan Thomas, to J. P. Donleavy, cheap beer, and noontime reruns of *The Andy Griffith Show*, Winder and I shared an enthusiasm for Phil. Gene raved about his poetry and teaching, often quoting him verbatim, and recommended I take one of his classes as soon as he returned from his first year abroad in Spain. As I remember it, enrollment in Phil's *undergraduate* creative writing seminar would be limited to twelve students, no more. Imagine that.

When September arrived with its copper haze and glare, I tentatively approached Phil's office in the humanities building—erected from previously existing architectural drawings intended for California State penitentiaries—to find him standing in the hallway smoking a cigarette.

Dressed in a plaid button-down sport shirt, burgundy sweater vest, white tennis shoes, and Levi's, Phil might have been a student himself. As if on cue, a rather patrician gentleman (who I later discovered was Wesley Byrd, chair of the Foreign Language Department) marched out of another office down the hall and addressed Phil as if he were a recalcitrant stable boy, informing everyone within a five-mile radius that smoking was not permitted in the halls and commanding Phil to stub out his cigarette forthwith.

After telling the guy to fuck off, Phil showed me into his second-story office with its window overlooking a strip of Bermuda grass decomposing in . the quad. Amazingly, he signed my add card.

Gene accompanied me to Phil's first class session that fall. I failed to dissuade him from sitting us in the front row.

My poem turned up in the first batch of dittos, those purple spirit–based copies that predated Xerox by decades. After Marsha and I married, I'd given my brother the kayak I'd made in the Sacramento Valley during my fourteenth winter. He had absolutely no use for such a thing, of course. The poem, which I would reproduce here to everyone's dismay if only I could locate it, contained such lines as "I find myself knee-deep in the backyard of my youth." I remember drafting it in the Fresno State cafeteria before punching in later as Community Hospital's only floating swing-shift orderly, at $2.25 an hour.

That evening, Phil read the poem and finished his comments by saying, "This shows talent." Gene turned to me and smiled. I remember little more except the feeling that in some way my life had utterly changed. It had.

It may be worth noting that in 1966, while still in his thirties, Phil was not yet the soft-spoken, ingratiating belletrist he has become today. In fact, his wit was wild and eviscerating, a bracing source of shock (*Awake!*) to all of us, an astounding and hilarious otherworldly amazement that focused our attention sharply on the business at hand: on the power of poetry, on the surprising possibility of living true lives. We shook with laughter even as we were being skewered. We loved it. We loved Phil Levine. I don't think anyone ever missed a class.

Phil would usually begin by reading a poem aloud to us—Jon Silkin's devastating "Death of a Son," for instance—followed by a brief and illuminating discussion. Then he'd move to the week's student poems, printed anonymously on a fresh stack of dittos. We were offered the opportunity to claim authorship by reading our own poems aloud. If the author declined, Phil would read the poem himself, read it carefully, as convincingly as it was ever likely to be read. Most of us kept quiet on such occasions. When Phil read our poems, we heard them truly for the first time. Imagine.

At each class meeting, he would return to us, without fail, the original typed copies of our poems with his extensive comments in red ink:

This word is a little too fancy, too literary. For me. It may o'erwhelm others.
This is a good, quiet and very suggestive ending.

This is dangling—it's the tree & not the display that's on its side.
This light, psychiatric word is awful & right.

Your work has improved a lot this semester: it moves better, it's about more while pretending to be about less, & it's seldom theatrical.

Each poem would also receive an overall assessment: the best were marked *good*; the decent stuff was *OK+*; then came *OK* and *OK–*; and finally, the legendary *argh!*, a distinction probably as rare as it was undesirable. I never saw one, except on the board during the first class meeting as Phil explained his grading system.

In the spring of 1968, Larry Levis and I drove in my '63 VW Bug from Fresno to UC Irvine for a weekend celebration called Manuscript Day, an extraordinary confabulation of poets and students. MS Day was also a chance for the fledging UCI Writing Workshop to attract attention and prospective applicants. In 1968, the university itself was only three years old.

There was a blur of parties, dinners, and readings all that weekend. Late Saturday night we wandered the beaches of Balboa Island, stopping wherever we saw a light on from a deck or an open window.

When the festivities had ended and we'd all somehow managed to avoid arrest, I eased the car back onto the Orange County freeways going north, with Phil as my only passenger. (Larry had taken a ride back the day before.)

After we coasted down the steep grade from Gorman and pulled over for gas outside of Bakersfield—we'd made it from Fresno to Laguna Beach and back as far as Mettler on four dollars worth of regular—Phil climbed into the back seat. As Aretha Franklin's "Respect" crackled from the AM radio, Phil stretched out as best he could for a nap.

When the tune ended, Phil's head reappeared in the rearview mirror, his hands grasping the back of the passenger seat.

"How long was I out? Half an hour?" he asked.

"Not quite," I answered.

He shuffled through some papers and asked whether I wanted to hear a new poem he'd finished the week before.

"Of course! I'd love to!"

As we cruised past the silos and cattle yards and swerved to avoid the dust devils crisscrossing the outskirts of Bakersfield, from the back seat of my battered VW, Phil read "They Feed They Lion" aloud for the first time.

Things were changing.

Over the years, Phil's poetry and friendship have given me back my life more times than I can count.

The summer I turned twenty-six, in 1972, desperate for steady jobs and the opportunity for both of us to teach, Marsha and I moved from Costa Mesa to Santa Catalina Island, where we began our stint at a doomed little boarding school in Toyon Bay, about a mile north by boat from Avalon Harbor. We were blessed with some marvelous students there, and we gave it everything we had. But we were simply not cut out for island boarding school life. Practically marooned, besieged by unimaginable difficulties, we eventually found ourselves bereft of health and hope and any reasonable prospects for the future. We signed on for a second year.

Each day before lunch, the mail was distributed in front of the cafeteria on a patch of grass under a grove of ancient eucalypti at the bottom of Toyon Canyon, within view of the sloping beach line, the narrow pier, and the water. One morning in March 1974, the school's business manager handed me a manila envelope containing a signed first edition of *1933*, with this inscription:

> For Bruce & Marsha, the poet and the painter fighting the only fight there on Mad Isle. I'm glad you have each other because there is nothing in the world that anyone could give you that would mean even an atom of that, but still it thrills me to give you this book born of people who sweated & loved & suffered as you have, & who like you kept carrying the stone up the hill because, my brother and sister, that's where our road goes. Love, Phil

As I read this even now, everything else simply stops, and only what matters most rises into perfect focus. At the moment, Marsha is painting beautifully and masterfully in the next room. Our daughter, now almost fifty, lives in a little yellow house barely nine minutes away. On the damp grass that morning almost forty years ago, I turned from the headmaster's announcements and admonitions and opened Phil's new book to this poem:

The Poem Circling Hamtramck, Michigan All Night in Search of You

He hasn't gone to work,
he'll never go back to work.
The wife has gone home, mad,
with the baby on one arm.
Swaying on his good leg,
he calls out to the bare bulb
a name and opens his arms.
The old woman,
the beer gone from her glass,
turns back to the bar.
She's seen them before
with hard knotted bellies,
with the bare white breasts of boys.
How many times has she stared
into those eyes glistening
with love or pain
and seen nothing
but love or pain.
Deep at night, when she
was coldest, he would always
rise and dress so as not
to miss the first streetcar
burning homeward, and she
would rock alone toward dawn.

If someone would enter now
and take these lovers—for they
are lovers—in his arms

and rock them together
like a mother with a child
in each arm, this man
with so much desire, this woman
with none, then it would not be
Hamtramck, it would not be
this night. They know it
and wait, he staring
into the light, she into
the empty glass. In the darkness
of this world, men
pull on heavy canvas gloves,
dip into rubber coats,
and enter the fires. The rats
frozen under the conveyors
turn to let their eyes
fill with dawn. A strange star
is born one more time.

The sudden infusion of such astonishing power and tenderness made the world somehow habitable again. We would make our future in it. This poem, and the whole of the book as I read and reread it, imparted a new resolve and clarity. For me, "The Poem Circling Hamtramck," like so much of Phil's work, performs a kind of secular miracle, where the fallen are lifted up, where those without hope are given a voice, where something of value becomes possible even in the face of "nothing / but love or pain." We were impelled to hold fast to what is best, to persevere, and to say our piece.

On the Teaching of Philip Levine

XOCHIQUETZAL CANDELARIA

I imagine there is a spectrum of poets. At one end are those who can pen lines effortlessly, the words practically leaping out of them as they describe a new cafe or light sifting through trees. And at the other end are those who can't believe they are writers because the writers they love seem like geniuses, whose words become light sifting through trees.

If you've ever worked with Phil Levine, you probably know what kind of poets gravitate toward him: writers concerned with the world around them, but equally concerned with the incantatory promise of a well-crafted line, the poem enacting and enabling our collective human spirit. Anything short, according to Phil, should be sent to the *Shit Creek Review*. In today's careerist culture, it is hard to find someone like Phil who is truly honest and willing to help young writers become the best writers they can be.

A fellow graduate from New York University's Creative Writing Program recently sent me a picture of our workshop members that she assumed I had taken because I wasn't in the photograph. Some of the group seem dazed and excited. The man who sits in front of Phil used to kiss his poems before workshop and say, "I'm sorry for what is about to happen to you." That man has gone on to achieve success as a poet, and I hope he feels that Phil's workshop, however challenging it might have felt, was worth it, the way one feels after a marathon, the heart pumping extra blood to all the extremities, the mind bathed in endorphins.

To change the course of poetry to come, I believe it's not enough to be a great poet; you have to be a great teacher, and we are indebted to Phil for how he has shaped poets—poets who don't even resemble one another, but if you look closely, you can see the imprint of the master teacher, like a tiny birthmark turned upside down or hidden behind the ear.

I think a true teacher knows how to push, inspire, humor, and lead—all things I have said and heard said about Phil Levine. I'm not saying Phil works for everyone; each student-teacher relationship requires both student and teacher to be tuned to the same frequency if they are going to hear each other. But if one has the opportunity to study with Phil, I'll say:

Because he takes you seriously
Because he won't believe in everything you write

Because he'll make you laugh
Because he's dead serious about poetry

Because his imagination is inspiring
Because he does not go in for ornamentation for its own sake

Because he has a wonderful command of narrative in poetry
Because he recognizes that some things can't be told

You can trust him.

When I say you can trust him, I mean he'll tell you what he thinks. He may use the term *meathead* now and again, but he recognizes when someone is trying, and he respects this as much as anything.

Phil once told me, in the kindest voice after carefully reviewing my words, "Sometimes we need to write another poem." I did, and the subsequent poem was a thousand times better than anything I had written that year in graduate school. If I hadn't trusted him, if I hadn't taken him at his word, who knows what kind of time I would have wasted worrying that I wasn't good enough? Instead, he gave me an opportunity to act, to learn, to take him and myself seriously. To have someone honestly respond to one's work with knowledge of the English poets, American poets, Spanish poets, and Mexican poets (to name a few), to have that person talk about poems with an understanding of history, politics, and imagination, is more than one can ask for.

I partially remember the abandoned poem; I was trying to write in iambic pentameter and there was a pond and my mother's cleavage in it. Honestly, my mother has never spent any significant time lying near any body of water. I think Phil knew I was hiding behind language in that poem. In retrospect, I suspect I was trying to write something I imagined *The New Yorker* might publish.

I know some poets follow the maxim "first thought, best thought," but Phil would remind us not to confuse first thought with first word. If you've ever heard a toddler talking, vowels flying, it can sound like pure inspiration and as good as poetry. But if you listen closely, that baby is trying, repeating, and perfecting—in short, revising.

In Phil's class, I learned a great deal about revision and how when a writer works really hard, he or she might find beauty, a great beauty, dwarfing individual concerns, so that it doesn't matter whether one writes a bad poem or ten bad poems. They get to live out their days with other bad poems, somewhere in Orange County, I suspect. More importantly, if one manages to write a good poem, perhaps it gets a life of its own, making some librarian, years from now, smile on an autumn day. So, a young writer tries her absolute best to write something that feels honed but honest. Or, as Phil says in his poem "The Simple Truth":

> Some things
> you know all your life. They are so simple and true
> they must be said without elegance, meter and rhyme,
> they must be laid on the table beside the salt shaker,
> the glass of water, the absence of light gathering
> in the shadows of picture frames, they must be
> naked and alone, they must stand for themselves.

I remember feeling lost before I entered Phil's class. Lost as a writer in Washington Square Park watching a perfectly formed man cut a figure eight on rollerblades by the Washington Arch. I thought, "What am I doing?" I was sure I was living on borrowed time back then because who gets to be a poet? My grandparents were migrant laborers, and I didn't grow up making sense of life through books. My mother didn't read a cookbook to prepare meals. My father, however, to this day has Cervantes's *Don Quixote* on the living room mantle; he's been reading and rereading it, perhaps his whole life. So there were books, but they rubbed elbows with our unpublished history, a chorus of feelings and insights reminding us that we are communal as well as solitary. My siblings and I learned by example, and at the end of the day we improvised stories, started by one child and finished by another, each of us attempting the most compelling line so as to narrate a scene or two. My sister Maria Christina and I spent hours on these stories, sometimes becoming identical characters (Leda 1 and Leda 2) creating a room of echoes—poems, really. Phil encouraged a return to this young imaginative impulse as well as movement toward the pickaxe and walnut trees of my Mexican-American heritage.

Phil would also remind us that poetry is a shared commitment, that we must listen and honor those around us, especially those who don't often make their way into poetry. Phil writes:

in the darkness
it's not easy to tell who is talking and who is listening, who giving,
who taking, who praying, who cursing. ("In the Dark")

Like hundreds are doing at this very moment in MFA programs around the country, I fell in love with a smart young man in Phil's workshop. However, we respected Phil's class so much that we never sat together, never let on for fear we might miss something. A great teacher can do this; he or she can imbue an experience with something sacred, something mutual, so that you check your identity at the door, if you know what is good for you. This is not to say that you ignore the very real implications of race, class, and gender, but you also don't assume you know the answers to your own life or life in general. You enter the great river, and you recognize mixtures, connections, and questions.

Some poets are satirical, some inspiring, others tender, inventive. Phil manages it all. He makes us laugh at our own shortcomings—not the simple kinds, but the serious shortcomings; he makes us laugh and, in so doing, can move us to imagination. I remember reading "On the Meeting of Garcia Lorca and Hart Crane" and enjoying his meta-jesting on what readers might expect when "poetic geniuses" meet, only to be reminded by the end of the poem how our imaginations can betray us, how cruel and detailed our thoughts can be. I have returned to that ending many times for comfort and courage. That is why I loved studying with Phil—because he understood that poetry is about offering a gift to the reader by sustaining contradiction. As a Chicana poet, this means the world to me. I left Northern California, my family, my job for New York City to be a poet at age twenty-five. And there was Phil, able to say without saying it: "Of course art is about sustaining contradiction, of course you're angry and laughing at the same time. Of course you come to language, history, and love with a skeptical heart. Poems should embody negative capability."

He acknowledged that it's okay to be obsessed with time and slippages, how one moment finds you years later and you don't know why. He acknowledged that it makes sense to highlight how poetry unfolds, promises, refuses, delivers, and how without it, you can feel completely lost.

I remember during one workshop Phil saying something about a line I had written and I knew he liked it and I felt my cheeks flush, felt the shine of poetry like golden leaves forever rising, forever falling.

It's beautiful whether or not you let it be

COLIN CHENEY

"Mystery? It's all a mystery."

I've flown back from Thailand for the funeral, suburban Philadelphia. The afternoon before the interment, we drive to the church three, maybe four times, delivering lilies, depositing and retrieving aunts and cousins, standing at the lectern imagining the nave full of family and strangers. Each trip, there and back, we pass a road-killed stag on the edge of the pike. Shoulders tense with rigor mortis, crown of antlers like undead coral on the macadam: the white belly unbroken. No one moves it from the road. Just before dusk, we drive home to linger in the kitchen with bourbon and beer, the ham and gratin potatoes a neighbor has left. When we pass the deer this time, two vultures lurk on the curb—petaled, Beauty rose faces; beaks suggesting an antler half-swallowed—shifting from foot to foot, waiting for the evening traffic to lull. So that they can approach, begin their work. Someone's sure to call someone to come and gather the deer now that the scavengers have arrived. I wonder how much of the beast they'll make part of themselves before the body is trucked away.

A father and son pry a gravestone out of the speedwell and wood sorrel. With sponge and toothbrush, they scrub dirt from the rills of eroded aleph and daleth and mem that the fishtail and lettering chisels left in the stone. Around them the green light and mosquito heat stretch through the retaken wilderness of the cemetery and out to the encircling wall. After taking the city, the soldiers had smashed the tombstones, sold the choice pieces to masons, and used the rest as paving stones—scattering the unearthed bones. Years later, many of the pieces were dug up, reclaimed and gathered together. And because it was impossible to restore and make each individual memorial whole again, someone began to take these shards of names and dates and created a mosaic of this breakage, this shattered evidence of lives.

"In this world / the actual occurs."

Dear Phil—

A guy came today to see about the mold in the room that'll be the baby's. It's currently my study. Every few weeks we find something else filmed with a fine, blue mold. A raincoat, my Brooklyn Dodgers cap, my damn books: I went at them with vinegar and baking soda, cursing. My friend Kathy, a cartoonist I know here, came over to translate, as my Thai is still terrible. An architect friend told us these were the guys who'd gone into homes after the flood waters finally fell in January, scrubbing away the two meters of fetid grime: factory runoff, decomposed fauna and flora, the mold blossomed in the greenhouse air. Turns out these guys don't know anything about mold— "I'm not a doctor," he says, however one says that in Thai. "I can't figure out what's in the air," Kathy translates. Fantastic.

Kathy was up 'til five this morning illustrating these poems by Nick Gulig, a Thai-American guy from Wisconsin here on a Fulbright. You'd like him. Serious about poetry, funny—digs boxing and dark, folk harmonies. He's writing fine, strange poems: "Your name is not // the world of things / I sing." He told me he'd never written about a city before living in Bangkok. Except the poems aren't about Bangkok. He's smart enough to let the poems unfold in an invented cityscape rather than this actual place, this city that I keep trying to build into my own poems. But maybe it took being here to create the pressure necessary to let his imagination work the memory—fragments of memory—into some new reality: the poem. Hell, that's probably not the way Nick thinks about it. But his poems remind me of something I'd forgotten, something you tried to teach me once about rejigging reality in a poem.

So Mari asked me to write something about what it's been like knowing you. I keep picturing one of those poetry events where the major and minor poets of America stand up to say things like "let me tell you about Phil Levine," or "what can I say about Philip Levine?" or "let me tell you about the Phil that I know." The inevitable speeches that'd follow would be beautifully wrought, saccharine, obsequious—sounding as though you're recently six feet under, even though you're sitting in the front row of the theater, bemused. I'll try to avoid that. Now, let me tell you about Philip Levine . . .

But what's happening in Fresno—are you getting good writing done? How are Franny's tomatoes? Tell me what you're reading—I'm still working my way through that collection of Lorca letters I found. Did he ever put on that puppet show in Granada, the one that was going to be true and beautiful, "something of art, which we need so badly." (This thing with the puppets is serious.)

Give my love to Franny, and hug Lorraine for me when you get back to Brooklyn. Anna and I are still looking for boy names if you have any kicking around the house.

Okay, I'm off to buy vinegar.

Love, Colin

> *unspoken,*
> *made of that dirt we call earth, the metal we call salt,*
> *in a form we have no words for*

I met Phil Levine for the first time after a reading he gave at the Tempel synagogue in the Kazimierz, Krakow's old Jewish Quarter. My friend Lorraine Doran and I had spent the day orienting ourselves to the city: the bones of the Krakow dragon (whale, mammoth, rhino), Mickiewicz's statue, our new favorite bar whose name (*Pierwszy lokal na Stolarskiej po lewej stronie idąc od Małego Rynku*) served as directions to the place, if you could read Polish. In the synagogue, as Phil read "The Mercy" and "The Simple Truth" and then listened as his poems were read again in Polish, I took down lines and stray thoughts to keep myself grounded and awake (jetlag, buffalo vodka) in the dim, almost vesper light.

I recollect only scraps of our conversation after the reading: salt mines, Franny's garden, Lorca. But I know we didn't get into what I'd been thinking about all day, since the morning talk he'd given on "Writing under the Sign of Memory." He'd talked about his decision to leave Detroit when he was twenty-six, how his friends had convinced him there were better ways to live. "I was being exploited," he said. But what had lingered with me was this: "My anger," he said, "my anger was so large that I couldn't find a technique to find my way out of it."

For him, this wasn't an abstraction—he needed to find a practice of poetry that would allow him to write beyond his anger. He wanted to write about the world he knew, the people he'd grown up with, worked alongside. But he hadn't yet found a way to write about this life—or, more, he hadn't found a way to let his imagination translate these memories and experiences into a new life, a new reality as poems. "Memory is all the imagination has to work on," he'd said, riffing on Coleridge. His memories of these men and women had been only snapshots before, he said. But then he gradually found a way to see these people "as noble as they truly were." Only then, he said, "could I write them as Caravaggios."

I'd carried the pressure of this thought as Lorraine and I had walked the city until we finally found ourselves in the cemetery. We lingered there, surrounded by the shattered gravestones carefully arranged into a mosaic wall. We listened to the leaves, the sound of metal on stone as two men levered a stone free of the undergrowth. And later, when we entered the dark quiet of the synagogue and settled inside the sphere that Phil's poems created, I tried to listen for and hold what shards of memory and lyric and imagination swerved toward me:

> mercy is something you can eat again and again
> (German soldiers in this synagogue, their silhouettes
>> (my grandfather's tweed jacket, cologne and sweat and rain
>> I began a career in root vegetables—
> (they do not see this language as the scrawl of frightened birds

In that temple used as a stable after its congregants—bankers, writers, mothers, grandfathers, industrialists, their children—were taken to be murdered a hundred kilometers out in the countryside at Birkenau and Auschwitz, I knew I hadn't found it yet. I hadn't found the technique that would allow me to shape these meanderings and impressions, these snapshots I had collected. I look back now and see myself full of fragments. I see myself seeking a physic that would allow me to craft some new mosaic from these broken pieces of the world. Even if that mosaic—these poems I hadn't yet found a way to write—left so much unanswered.

"Too much bird bird bird in the poem. Too many birds," Phil is saying about the poem at hand: my poem.

We're sitting around the table in a windowless room off Washington Square. Windowless: but there are portraits of poets where windows might be. Each of our faces betrays something: wariness, sly joy, a desire to take a swing at the poem.

The poem seems to want to be about watching a friend cook dinner as she describes climbing a mountain to witness a sky burial. But things are not going well. "No, that person never felt that," Phil says of a bit of dialogue I'd invented for this soul I'd shanghaied into the poem. "It's damn confusing," he says. "You've got to rearrange the poem's reality."

"I want more from this speaker," Phil says of my failing poem. I had tried to describe a "sky burial," the Parsi ceremony where the dead are offered to the vultures of the Himalayan plateau. But I didn't understand what I was writing about, not quite. "You have to be pretty angry to feed someone to the birds," Phil says, confused about what I'd described because I was confused about what I was describing, trying to evoke. "The poem loses its anger because of the ending"—I hadn't realized it was an angry poem.

"You need to read Hardy's 'Transformations,'" he tells me. "Have you read that?" I hadn't. He quotes Hardy:

So, they are not underground,
But as nerves and veins abound
In the growths of upper air

—No. I hadn't found the technique to say whatever it was I trying to say. Not yet.

A few months later, I'll try again and will write a new poem in dialogue with the failure of this first poem. While still wide-ranging, still asking the reader to tack between disparate landscapes and narrative fragments, this new poem, "Ars Poetica with Vulture," will take the difficulty of knowing as its form, its lyrical meandering shape. Writing this poem, I will try to keep in mind the last thing Phil says about this poem on the table before us in this room full of poets trying to figure out what kind of poet they want to be, the poets we are. I'd written:

Would you want
to be given to a bird, hear creatures crating psalms
of your flesh in their bodies? This is grotesque
& beautiful, but only if you let it be.

"No," Phil says, looking at me and then back to the poem, "that's wrong. It's beautiful whether or not you let it be."

The deer was gone the next morning when we drove to my grandfather's funeral. In the cemetery behind the church, we stood in the cold, winter light as the priest said his words. A lieutenant commander in the navy presented my grandmother with the ensign, said something to her I couldn't hear. The ground was frozen: we would need to wait until spring before interring his ashes. Before we went inside, I saw two vultures circling something a ways off, above the empty deciduous trees.

During the years I worked in New York City, my grandfather wrote me letters. He'd ask about my rooftop garden work, describe a piece of furniture he was rebuilding for an upcoming antique show out on the Main Line. He'd give me stories about the German and Hmong immigrants he'd worked alongside in the hammer and ax factory outside Philadelphia, men with nicknames like "Sleeping Jesus," "Snowball," "Battle of the Marne," and "Suckie." (He once included a clipping from the *Inquirer*: "Poetry is finding fans—even cash.") From memory, he'd illuminate the letters with hand-drawn diagrams of drop forges, maps of the assembly line, sketches of the antique Empire and Late Empire chests of drawers, fiddleback chairs, or butler's desks he'd find abandoned in fields and try to restore: sanding them down, scraping away coats of paint, dovetailing-in pieces of walnut or cherry to replace what had been lost, broken, or destroyed by ignorance and neglect.

"When you lose that avenue to the past," Phil wrote me in an e-mail after the funeral, after I'd returned to Bangkok, "it's usually gone forever." But, of course, poems can also be a kind of wayfinding into that irrevocably lost past. They give shape to that absence: a map built of fragments. The imagination, Coleridge writes, "dissolves, diffuses, dissipates, in order to recreate." So perhaps fragments are all we have: of memory, yes, but also of language, and what Thoreau calls "the actual world." And we work from there—sketching, scraping away, dovetailing—until we find a technique to give new life to what can't be restored.

After the funeral, before I fly back to Thailand, I meet Phil, Franny, and Lorraine at Teresa's, a Polish place in Brooklyn Heights. We order pierogies, blintzes, Żywiec beer, chianti. We laugh a lot. We argue about something and some of us grow quiet for a little while. I try to talk about living in Bangkok but can't quite find the words. Say I am trying to write an essay about the flood, the riots and fires, about the lèse-majesté laws, about what you can't say. I feel like I might be getting close to it. We talk about parents and grandparents. We don't talk about poems.

Before Lorraine and I walk back to the subway, I tell Phil and Franny that Anna is pregnant, that we're having a baby in May. Phil asks whether we know if it's a boy or girl. We want to wait, I say, keep it a mystery. He smiles and shakes his head, "A mystery? It's all a mystery."

It's beautiful whether or not I let it be.

They Feed They Lion and Me

MIKE CLIFTON

It was David St. John who got me in my first workshop with Philip Levine at Fresno State. I was scared shitless. My roommate, an English major too, and already teaching high school, had told me—several times over—all the horror stories about how tough a teacher Phil was. David kept saying, *come on, come on—I can get you in.*

So I let him talk me into it and kept thinking I'd hyperventilate that first session of the workshop. The poem—the fragment I finally managed to squeeze out—wasn't any good and I knew it. But it had one decent image at the end, I thought; it was the best I could do.

Phil, thank God, read our poems himself that week; I couldn't have done it. After he finished reading mine, there was a long pause, and he finally said, "This sounds like something out of Walt Disney." I thought, holy shit it's true—everything they say about him is true, and I've just made the biggest mistake I've ever made in my life, hearing similar comments roll out ahead of me week after week of the semester. And then he said, *that last image is good.*

That was what Phil did: he'd rip you a new one over everything in the poem that wasn't good and then he'd point out the single line, sometimes the single half-line, worth saving. He was always right.

We were all meeting that semester in Roberta Spear's apartment, Phil included, right across the street from campus. Every week one of us was delegated to bring a bottle of wine, one of the big, cheap ones we could afford like Red Mountain—five dollars for a half-gallon of really bad stuff. So it was possible that by the time it came to read my own poem, my hand wouldn't shake so hard when I tried to recite it from memory.

And we got better. We got better than I ever thought we'd get. I was surprised and couldn't tell whether the other students were getting better, too, but Phil would say things, very quietly, in the middle of a conversation, like "writing poetry is the most important thing you'll ever do." No fanfare, no special emphasis. The conversation would go on to other things. He was the first person I'd ever met who was completely serious about poetry, and that dedication of his changed everything I thought about it. I think that was true for all of us. Musicians know this: when you play with someone better than you, someone really good, you find yourself playing better than you thought you could.

One night we were all talking about the poets we were reading at the time. All of us were reading Pablo Neruda, César Vallejo (in translation), James Wright, or W. S. Merwin; at least I was. We all gave Phil a hard time when he said he was rereading Whitman. We were young and thought there was little point in reading older poets; Phil was adamant that we had a lot to learn from Whitman if we paid attention.

Later that semester in the old science lecture hall, Phil read "They Feed They Lion" for the first time. We were early, just hanging out, because we'd come back to campus solely for the reading, and Allen Jacobson came in, pale, and said, "They just killed four students at Kent State." It was devastating news: I'd grown up with that image of the National Guardsmen walking the little black girls to school in the South; I'd always thought somehow that the people who hated hippies and antiwar protestors were just crackers, the same ones screaming at the little girls—that the Guard would never shoot *us*. And then Phil read that poem about rage building slowly, while I was beginning to understand not only that they would, that they just had, but also that he was right about the power of catalogs. Both together, the poem and the news, rocked me. He's always been a great reader, but I don't remember him ever reading any better than that.

When I graduated from high school in Fresno in 1967, I remember being upset at first that I couldn't afford to go to a University of California campus like so many of the people I'd gone to school with. And then David dragged me into Phil's workshop. If Phil hadn't been blue-collar, I probably wouldn't have listened. But I have this notion now, deeply held, that poetry is the one thing you never fool around with, that if you're going to write it, you write with all the art and honesty you can bring. I think I learned that from Phil.

A Real Fact

MICHAEL COLLIER

In a 1974 interview with Wayne Dodd and Stanley Plumly, Philip Levine refers
to Yvor Winters as "my teacher," and then, responding to a confirming follow-up
question, "Winters was a teacher of yours?," he has a second thought: "That's
an odd word. He was an acquaintance." *Acquaintance* seems an equally odd
word given the careful and detailed description of Winters and his teaching
methods in Levine's warm but uncompromising essay about his time with
Winters at Stanford, "The Shadow of the Big Madrone," although reading the
essay, you can see Levine's point. In the interview, Levine describes Winters
as "a brilliant reader of poetry. Even when you didn't agree with his evaluation
of a poem, it was clear he could read it very carefully." But "he was terribly
clumsy. He wanted to be kind and he didn't quite know how" . . . and "he was
very unperceptive on the level of relationships with people." By temperament,
Levine found Winters's model as a teacher alien and vexing. Even so, Levine
learned essential things from Winters, not only about poetry, but perhaps
more important and necessary, about himself. Reading "The Shadow of the
Big Madrone" and another essay about mentors, "Mine Own John Berry-
man," in which Levine compares Berryman's teaching with Robert Lowell's,
both of whom he worked with at Iowa, you get a clear sense that what Levine
values in teachers is their humanity and their ability to relate to the human-

ity of those they are charged to teach. Related to this, I think, is the ability to be honest and truthful in appraising others and yourself. Perhaps the most telling thing Levine says about Winters in this regard is how Winters, who was almost thirty years older than Levine, wanted to show him how he used to box. "He was a frustrated prizefighter," Levine tells his interviewers, "and he hadn't the vaguest idea of how to box . . . under all this mind business was a man with an unhappy body."

At the Bread Loaf Writers' Conference in 1986 (the closest I ever got to being a workshop student of his), Levine gave a lecture in which, among other things, he talked about the difference between teaching at Princeton and his alma mater, Wayne State. Princeton students were apt to become emotionally undone when he critiqued their poems, whereas Wayne State students responded with, "Fuck you Levine." The comparison here of Detroit working-class students with privileged Ivy Leaguers is similar to his comparison of Berryman, a university fellowship student, albeit Ivy League, and underrecognized poet, with Lowell, a Boston Brahmin and Pulitzer Prize winner. Levine's comparisons weren't merely intended to make digs at the privileged, although you might guess where his sympathies lay. Both stories offered a parable about the importance of character and temperament. There was really nothing in Levine's illustrations to say the parable couldn't have worked the other way around, that is, with Lowell as the magnanimous, passionate, fair-minded, and interested teacher or the Princeton students stubbornly standing up for their own work.

The waiters at Bread Loaf that summer—the cohort of young writers who serve food in the conference dining hall to more than two hundred people and whose esprit de corps sets them apart from most of the participants while simultaneously making them subservient to everyone—took Levine's talk to heart. During dinner, a few days later, a group of waiters approached his table, and once they had his attention, they peeled off their aprons to reveal red T-shirts with big black block lettering—FUCK YOU LEVINE. They had made one for him to wear and he put it on without hesitation. I'm not sure whether it was one of the waiters who took the photograph afterward, nor do I remember how a copy of it came into my possession, but it is one of my most revered icons, and for years I had it thumb-tacked on the wall above my writing desk. I kept it there as a reminder that writing is not primarily about receiving praise and affirmation from others. We do it to please ourselves, primarily, and as such, we must be the final critics and editors of our poems.

This is one of the attributes of Levine and his work that has always inspired me: a belief in self-reliance, an ultimate existential stance in relationship to the art we make, which gets translated into a restlessness with the medium itself. He wasn't arguing for pigheadedness, even though while recounting Winters's boxing skills Levine said, "I could have beaten Yvor Winters with my head," but rather for clarity of purpose and single-mindedness. Also, and this is something of an extrapolation, Levine asks for an ongoing self-scrutiny and openness, an understanding of who we are not just as writers, but as human beings. In this regard, I'm reminded of something that William Meredith said about Muriel Rukeyser—that her life and art were seamless, "you couldn't get a knife between those two things."

At Bread Loaf that summer, I had asked to be assigned to Levine's workshop, but wasn't. Fortunately, Edward Hirsch, a good friend, was at the conference and because Levine and he had known each other for a number of years, I had an introduction, so to speak. Toward the end of session Levine asked whether he could look at some of my poems. I gave him the sheaf of six poems I had sent in with my application. Of course, I hoped he would say something to me about the poems while the conference was in progress, but I didn't expect it. The pace of things at Bread Loaf is such that if you have any extra time you are likely to use it to lie down in your room with the shades drawn and a cool washcloth on your forehead, so I was taken aback when he returned the sheaf the next day not only with comments and suggestions neatly written on each page, but also with a handwritten letter attached.

What I considered the best poem of the batch, Levine found "the least satisfying." "Yet," he tried to console me, "the idea (if that's the word) it presents" was worthy. In reference to the idea, whose main image was the eyepiece of a telescope, he said, "I think I should be scared a bit more by how easily we all lose things and how impossible it is to regain them once we lose the proper focus." For me, a comment like that, which allowed me to see his mind and heart responding to the inspiration (if that's the word) behind the poem was as important as the suggestion he made about revising the poem's ending: "This is getting a bit too neat for me. I'd be content with only the roommate as the closing device." Or about the use of *lover*. "For me," he noted, "this word seems odd, European, Jamesian?" When writing the poem, I had struggled with that word but gave up when I couldn't find a substitute. It was a soft spot in the poem and he'd easily found it. Although his observations about diction and the ending of the poem were accurate and helpful, they were very different from his musing on the poem's so-called idea. This observation was not only speculative, but it demonstrated how intelligence ("mind business") works in an expansive way with emotion and feeling.

And this expansiveness is one of the qualities I initially responded to in Levine's work when I encountered it in 1971 in *Naked Poetry*, a copy of which had been given to me by my freshman composition teacher, Gabriel Rico, at Santa Clara University.

For me, and I suspect for many other writers of my generation, *Naked Poetry*, published in 1969, was like a Rosetta Stone for understanding mid-twentieth-century contemporary American poetry. Starting with Kenneth Rexroth, who was born in 1905, the anthology ends with the editors, Stephen Berg and Robert Mezey, who were born in 1934 and 1935, respectively. In the anthology's chronology, Levine follows James Wright and precedes Sylvia Plath, who precedes Gary Snyder. Interestingly, the selection of Levine's poems is formally more like Plath's than Wright's, and yet the direct, speechlike quality of the diction and the stripped-down and sincere tone of the speaker are so much closer to Wright's that you might look past Levine's careful and unobtrusive use of syllabics and rhyme. I responded intuitively to these formal arrangements in "Silent in America," "Baby Villon," and "Commanding the Elephants" and viscerally to the searching, probing, restless nature of their speakers. In each poem there was an active tension as the form tried to contain, but not tame, the speaker's varying emotions of anger, tenderness, confusion, and joy. Especially vivid were the poems about Fresno. Their landscape was similar to that of Phoenix, Arizona, where I was born and raised, which then was still very much an agricultural town with neighborhoods built on former cotton and melon fields or in citrus groves, all of which were being gobbled up by a senseless, unrelentingly consumer-driven, air-polluting, leisure-retirement-industry development.

Although I was only eighteen when I read Levine in *Naked Poetry* and truly didn't know what it was I was reading, not the way I would even two or three years later, his poems gave me, more than any other poet I had read at the time, an example of how to write as directly and forthrightly as possible about what it was like to be alive in the middle of the twentieth century. There was an audacity as well as a trustworthiness about the speaker in the poems that suggested, *what I'm saying, what I've learned and discovered is the truth, but it's only part of the truth. The other part of the truth is what I don't know, can't know, and will likely never know.*

What I experienced in my first encounter with Levine has stayed with me throughout the years as a kind of encouragement, but also as a demand, an exhortation, and an obligation to ensure that the poem justifies itself by the rigor of its utterance and by the truth at which it arrives. This stance toward poetry is partially encapsulated in the letter he attached to the poems I'd given him at Bread Loaf. The overall tone of the letter is one of supportive solidarity. Its opening is slightly apologetic ("I felt a bit odd about what I'd done in scratching my crabbed & sometimes crabby words across your poems") because he realized belatedly that all of the poems I had given him were being published in my first book. After which, he writes, the "real fact" is "above all things" what "I value in imaginative writing." And then, perhaps as a cautionary, "I just know you would know when to say, 'Eat Shit,' and when not to." In closing the letter, I love how he avoids, actually repudiates, the empty convention of predicting great things for the work of a young poet. He considers the gesture "impertinent": "What do I know about what you want to do & what life will make you want to do. If you have a glimmer you have far more than I did at your age or have now at my own." Belief in the "real fact," the necessity to say "Eat shit," and then the honest recognition of uncertainty ("What do I know? . . .") are three priceless and extremely useful gifts Levine offered. They were given simply and modestly. I feel incredibly fortunate to have received them first from his poems and then from Philip Levine himself.

Trust the Poet

Reflections on *Phil Levine at Three Universities*

NICOLE COOLEY

Brown University, 1985

"Trust the poem, not the poet," Phil Levine told our poetry writing class that spring, years ago, when I was his student at Brown University. "Why would you believe the poet anyway?"

But I believed Phil. I had just turned eighteen. It was my freshman year in college. I wrote down everything he said, read and reread his work, and memorized his poems. I carried his recently published *Selected Poems* in my book bag around campus until the cover fell off in pieces.

Phil's class was different from any class I had ever taken, or have taken since. At Brown, creative writing classes were infamously difficult to get into: at the first class meeting students did a writing exercise in a blue exam book and were chosen on the basis of what they wrote. For a university that prided itself on not requiring grades and having an innovative curriculum, this was a curious choice. The first class was thus very anxiety provoking for all prospective students: the classroom would be crowded with students writing furiously in blue books for an hour as if they were taking a final exam on the first day of the semester.

On the first day of Phil's class, he told everyone who showed up that they were in the class. There were no blue books. Phil just started talking about poetry. We were all shocked, then thrilled. His spirit of inclusion set the tone for the rest of the semester. Our class included not only undergraduates, but also a professor from the Psychology Department and a songwriter who played his poems on his guitar. Discussion was lively and wide-ranging. Many of us went on to become poets and publish books.

Yet, what was most important about this class was that Phil gave us permission to be writers and showed us how important poetry was. He encouraged us to write about what mattered most to us and helped us to see that poetry did not have to be focused on the beautiful. As he would write later in his wonderful poem "Coming Close," about a factory, "Make no mistake, the place has a language." Phil gave me—and still gives me—permission to write about Louisiana or Queens or any place I've lived. He taught us that where we were from had value and showed us that part of our responsibility as poets was to record the places and people who were disappearing, who were already gone.

Phil gave me permission in another crucial way: "Just write," he told me. "Stop worrying so much about being a writer." He told me to write about people I knew, about places I had been, and to quit thinking about where I would publish my poems.

The University of Iowa, 2011

In the summer of 2011, when I attended the celebration weekend of the seventy-fifth anniversary of the Iowa Writers' Workshop, Phil was a featured speaker. On the final evening of the reunion, a dinner was held that included a writer from each decade of the workshop. Representing the decade of the fifties, Phil stood and read part of his wonderful essay "Mine Own John Berryman." Focused on his experience as a student of Berryman's in Iowa City in 1954, the piece is a beautiful reflection not only on Berryman, but also on the teacher-student relationship in the creative writing classroom.

Phil writes: "In spite of his extraordinary sense of humor, the key to Berryman's success as a teacher was his seriousness. No doubt his amazing gift for ribaldry allowed him to devastate our poems without crushing our spirits." This was so true of my experience as Phil's student. When he said to my class when I was an undergraduate, "I heard better language than this on the bus coming over" or "Our friend has given us a very clever and intelligent piece of writing, and if he continues doing this there's a good chance he'll never write a real poem," all of us were challenged to work harder, to move our poems to new levels.

Listening to Phil read from the essay in 2011, I was reminded again of his wonderful teaching and how much we all learned from him and how I still carry the lessons of Phil's class with me, nearly thirty years later.

Queens College–The City University of New York, 2011

Each semester, in my job at Queens College, I start my undergraduate and graduate poetry writing classes by assigning Phil's poems. I can't imagine a more important or necessary poetry with which to begin each semester.

On our public urban university campus where more than 129 languages are spoken, our undergraduates are often first-generation college students, often immigrants, who work full time. In fact, Queens College is much like Wayne State, where Phil was a student, and Fresno State, where Phil taught for many years.

When they read Phil's book *What Work Is*, my students are always stunned. Over and over, they tell me they had no idea that work—the kind they do, the kind their families do—could be the subject of poetry. In Phil's poems, they find a reflection of their own worlds: factories, unemployment lines, and people looking for and waiting for work in different landscapes.

For the graduate students in our MFA program, Phil's lessons are perhaps even more important. MFA student Drew Biscardi explained: "When I read Philip Levine's poems, I am reminded that poems are everywhere around us in the seemingly mundane and the overlooked. He reminds us as poets that we need to be ever ready, looking deeply at all the everyday chaos around us for the poetry that is contained in it, acknowledging that the plainest of moments and the humblest of people hold something deeply beneath their surfaces." This is what I most want to teach my students, what I take from being Phil Levine's student: to write poems that look beneath the surface of the world.

At Queens in 2011, we invited Phil to read as part of our "New Salon in Queens" series, cosponsored with the Poetry Society of America, not only because he is a Pulitzer Prize winner, not only because he was the United States Poet Laureate, not only because he is the author of eighteen books of poems, but because his work and his presence show us how much poetry matters, how much our lives and the places we are from matter, and how much we can trust poetry to teach us about ourselves and our world. The lessons Phil taught me when I was his student—the lessons he continues to teach me now—have made me the writer, teacher, and reader that I am today. To pass these lessons that I learned from Phil on to my own students is an enormous gift.

Birth in a Poetry Position

On Philip Levine

KATE DANIELS

The first time I heard Philip Levine read his poetry was at the University of Virginia, my alma mater, in the early 1980s, where I had recently been hired as a lecturer in creative writing. Levine's national literary reputation was just beginning to rise, and he read to an overcrowded group in the auditorium of the biology building. The only previous event I had attended there had been a screening of a (horrifyingly realistic) film called "Birth in a Squatting Position." That fact seemed only random and irrelevant as I entered the auditorium that evening and snagged a last seat.

At the time of Levine's reading, I was a year out of my MFA studies in poetry at Columbia University where I had worked with Stanley Kunitz, Amiri Baraka, Joseph Brodsky, Donald Justice, and others. Levine himself had taught at Columbia the spring before I entered, and a terrible rumor was circulating when I first arrived. In his poetry workshop, so it was said, Levine had been a ruthless craft master who had made every single student in the workshop cry. "Even the *men*," we were told with emphasis. Then we would look around furtively, searching for a certain second-year student who had just had poems accepted by *The New Yorker* and *Poetry*. He was a large, bearded, beefy man with insolent posture and angry eyes who stalked through the corridors of Dodge Hall as if it were the OK Corral. We were both dazzled by and terrified of him. "*Him? Even him?*" we would query each other. What kind of a writer was capable of reducing a young poet god-in-the-making like him to tears?

Another rumor was snail-mailing about during that pre-Internet era that concerned a truly fearsome writer at the University of Alabama who sometimes taught his workshop with a handgun laid casually on the tabletop right beside his students' manuscripts. *Him* we could imagine bringing someone to tears, but not Philip Levine, who had recently published a charmingly marvelous essay called "Letters from a Young Poet" and who (as far as I could tell from the few poems of his I had read at that point) was a straight-shooting, unpretentious, un-macho type of writer, secure in his identity as a left-wing family man and advocate for the economically, socially, and politically oppressed. Levine seemed absolutely not a member of what my poet (girl)friends and I came to call the "Narcissistic American Male Poet–Dominated Crash-and-Burn School of Workshop Criticism." Still, the story about making my fellow students cry made me wary.

I was sure of very little in those days, but I was certain that I did not want to meet the man who made serious young poets cry in front of each other. At great personal cost, I had schooled myself *not* to cry from an undergraduate poetry workshop with the shockingly direct Louise Glück. I think I was probably always more or less about to cry in those days. Not about poetry, though. I was avid for criticism and could dish it out and take it alike. Whenever the knives cut too close, I sucked it up and made sure I was alone before starting to sob. Poetry—reading it, trying to write it, loving it—was really the only place I felt at all strong and authentic. I felt most real when I was reading and writing poetry. Perhaps it was the unconscious desire not to threaten that internal respite that held me back from reading Levine's poetry while at Columbia, or in that first year after graduate school.

At UVA a man named E. D. Hirsch was chairman of the English Department when Levine came to Charlottesville for his reading that year. At the time, Hirsch was just beginning to articulate the idea that would make him famous in academia. He called it "cultural literacy," a pedagogical plan designed to forestall emerging theories of cultural diversity that argued for core knowledge to be transmitted through identical curricula taught to all schoolchildren everywhere. There was a rumor about him, too: having been assailed as a kind of Nazi because of some aspect of his always controversial work, Hirsch was said to have actually laughed off the insult, and had even

48

repeated it to others. What kind of man did *that*, those of us in the nontenure nether regions of the department wondered.

Of course, it is easy this far past this moment in time—my first Philip Levine poetry reading—to anticipate the metaphorical car wreck that was approaching in the form of the decision by the culturally patrician Hirsch not to attend the reading by the anarchist poet Levine. But I didn't see it then. Thus, I was blindsided when Levine took the podium, and rather than effusively thanking everyone, per usual, for inviting him to the hallowed grounds of that great democrat Thomas Jefferson began, instead, to speak familiarly of E. D. Hirsch—a senior colleague almost everyone in the department either cowed away from or genuflected in front of.

"Out on the street," Levine said offhandedly, in a rough voice and Detroit accent, "I just met the chairman of the English Department." It was the first time I had heard a poet speak in such a tone. My god, he sounded like Groucho Marx! I was used to a very different rhetorical model for poetry readings—respectful, somewhat grave, even reverential. Readings often felt like going to church. Among those of us who knew Don Hirsch, there was nervous tittering.

"The chairman was driving his Porsche," Levine went on. "And he stopped beside me, and said he was sorry, but he couldn't come to the reading tonight."

More nervous laughter.

"And when I said, yeah, why not?" Levine said, his tone aggressively condescending, "the chairman said, uh, I have to go to the—uh dentist. And then he took off in his Porsche."

At that point, the auditorium dissolved in laughter. Like a dog who had marked his territory, Levine was liberated to begin his reading. With this public airing of the chairman's dismissal of contemporary poetry, he had cleared out the rarefied area usually reserved for poetry in academia at that time. In place of privilege, Levine had constructed a brand new space for American poets and poetry: backtalk from urban streets thronged with culturally diverse people who all had their own ideas on language and meaning, and who had the guts to proclaim that their utterances–*their* experiences, *their* lives—had a place in American poetry, and that they were ready to claim it.

And suddenly, my fetal poet self—southern white working-class female, product of generations of bewildered, uneducated, disenfranchised people struggling to eke out a minimal living from the piney flats of Tidewater, Virginia—found herself tumbling out of the womb into a new world. Somehow

49

the brief piece of performance art Levine had engaged in had shown me how intimidated I had felt by the discourse and ritual of academia, and even how I had agreed to my own marginalization in the lush world of English literature that I had come to love—the world that, paradoxically, had delivered me from the socioeconomic fate of my forebears.

Levine's brief performance—his comedic poke at the many presumptions of academic life and so-called cultural literacy—showed me that I had somehow agreed to my own marginalization: that I could be a poet only if I gave up the sharp edges of myself and tried to sound like something I wasn't, someone who had lived a life that neither I nor my people had ever had a chance to live. The class rage that I had been holding back (I now saw) for the entire length of my life forced its way out of me. It was time to be born.

I have no memory of the rest of the reading. I *do* remember afterward going to the library and checking out all of Levine's books, piling them up in chronological order, and reading them straight through. There I met my people, disguised as his people. I knew at that point that I had found the materials of my writing life. What I did *not* know was that I was soon to meet Philip Levine, to find in him a lasting mentor who would read each of my books of poetry in manuscript, who would recommend me for fellowships and tenure, that we would give readings together, that I would meet him and Fran in both their homes in Fresno and Brooklyn, that he would play tennis with my husband on courts all over the East Coast (culminating in a visit to the 2011 U.S. Open to watch Rafael Nadal play), and that we would be colleagues at Vanderbilt University in 1995 when he won the Pulitzer Prize. Later, my colleague Mark Jarman and I would bring him back to Vanderbilt for a celebration of his seventy-fifth birthday that Levine insisted focus more on his poet friends than on him. We—Chris Buckley, Peter Everwine, Ed Hirsch, Galway Kinnell, Dorianne Laux, Paul Mariani, Gerald Stern, Mark, and I—had a grand time.

I could probably write forever about the poetic, personal, and political importance of Philip Levine in my life. But I'll settle for closure by sharing the end of a long poem I wrote in homage to him. I called it "Crowns," but I could as easily have called it "Midwife," in tribute to the poet who gave birth to me.

I'll love Levine forever . . . [because he] would have understood my uncles,
enthroned on plastic-covered kitchen chairs patched with tape,
their work boots kicking up mucky clouds of chiggery dirt,

their pickups parked nearby, shotguns in the rack,
sucking on cheap beers and harsh cigarettes,
their nails starved by nicotine to yellow curls, the car grease
embedded permanently in the creases of their hands.

When I met him, he was such a mensch, massive
in my mind, but in the flesh, something touching
about his shoulders in the worn tweed jacket, something
vulnerable in his feet in an ordinary pair of soiled, white sneakers.
He opened his mouth to laugh, one side rising up
like it does, in that derisive gesture that seems, at first, a sneer,
and I remembered my mother flexing back her lips to remove
delicately, with two stained fingers, just so, a fleck of tobacco
lodged between her teeth, and saw again my father flossing at the table
with the torn off cover of a paper book of matches,
then stubbing out his butt in the yellowed, oily pod of broken yolk
that was hemorrhaging across his breakfast plate.

I can face those images now without the shame
I carried in the days before the poetry of Phil Levine
liberated me. I can look at anything now, because I keep
his picture in my mind and his poems in my pocket.
I can stand my life because I wear the crown he constructed
for people like me—grocery checkers, lube jobbers, truck drivers,
waitresses—all of us crowned with the junkyard diadems
of shattered windshields and rusty chains, old pots
with spit tobacco congealing inside, torn screen doors
and gravestones in the front yard, just five short steps from life to death . . .

So there is my family with their broken beer bottles
and patched shoes, their mutts chained in a back yard
carved from a stingy pine woods, on cheap land
out near the county dump where the air swells with the perfume
of trash, a circle of them playing poker in a trailer somewhere
in the woods, or razoring the state decal from the windowshield
of a ransacked wreck to transfer to my brother's car.
Or cleaning fish on the back porch and throwing the guts
to the tick-clogged dogs, or frying venison in a cast-iron pan

and stinking up the house with that heavy smell, showing
the buck's big balls in a plastic cannister that once held salt.
Or burning tires in a field some autumn, scumming
the sky with a smoky, cursive black they can't even read
but inhale poisonously again and again.

And there I am, walking along tolerantly now, with Phil Levine,
his poems in my pocket, his good rage gathered in my heart
and I can love them again, the way I did in the years before
I saw what they were and how the world would use them
and accepted the fact they were incapable of change.
We're in a field I used to love, a redbone coonhound running ahead
her ears dragging the edges of the goldenrod till they are tipped
in pollen, like twin paintbrushes dipped in gilt. And the world
is hunting dogs and country music and unschooled voices
bending vowels and modest kitchen gardens where late tomatoes
are tied up with brownish streamers of old nylon hose.
The vast way your chest expands when the sun gradually sets
in mid-fall in central Virginia. The tobacco barns glimmering
in last light, the chinks darkening now, the slats solidifying at the close of day
and your mind opening up like the pine forest swishing fragrantly overhead
way up in the dark that is coming, but remains for the moment beauti-
fully at bay.

What We Were Doing Was Work

BLAS MANUEL DE LUNA

1

I don't know how one gets so lucky. There you are, having a not-so-good life in Madera, thinking that it's always going to be that way: not so good. Little by little, however, poetry invades your life. It starts with DeWayne Rail, one of Phil's old students, in an American Literature class at Fresno City College in the spring of 1989. He introduces us to Whitman, and you fall in love with poetry the way that DeWayne is in love with poetry. Of course, now you want to try to write the stuff, even though you've never written a word of poetry before and you might not be any good at it. You take DeWayne's workshop the next semester, and he tells you about Phil, about how Phil had been a teacher of his, about how he had been a great one.

That was it. You're in Fresno, in love with poetry, learning to write it from a teacher who had been Phil's student. After that workshop, you feel like you're on the team, the Fresno poetry team. You feel like maybe your life has been saved.

2

Phil created the poetry context at California State University, Fresno. What I mean is that what we consider to be Fresno poetry—the culture, the community, the high standards, the poetry itself—starts with him. It's in the air.

The culture that exists at CSU, Fresno, is pretty amazing, and you know that going in. You can find a history of that community in a few anthologies—*Down at the Santa Fe Depot: 20 Fresno Poets, Piecework: 19 Fresno Poets,* and *How Much Earth: The Fresno Poets*—and in all of the poetry that has come out of the poetry workshops and out of the city. The standards are high and you will have to find the best version of yourself and your writing to live up to those standards, and you also know that before you even set foot on campus. And it all has to do with Phil.

3

It's 1991, the spring semester at CSU, Fresno. I was enrolled in English 161, the advanced undergrad poetry workshop with Phil Levine. I was also taking the translation workshop that he was co-teaching with Jose Elgorriaga. I didn't know it at the time, but Phil was soon to retire, so I was in some of the last classes that he would ever teach in Fresno.

I was a kid, twenty-one years old, probably one of the youngest members of that translation workshop. Because I was both shy and a little scared, I sat in the row closest to the door, near the front, my desk angled back toward where Jose and Phil sat.

From my seat off to the side, it felt like I was watching two great jazz musicians taking turns soloing. Jose would tell us when our translations were right on and when we were "making it up," and Phil would make connections between the translation being workshopped and the great body of poetry in Spanish. I remember the both of them laughing all of the time, taking great pleasure in the originals, in our sometimes successful translations, and in each other.

4

The workshop was an undergrad workshop. This was Philip Levine. We all knew that his poetry was amazing, that it was built to last. He had already won many of the big awards. He could have cruised through that class in a lower gear, and we probably wouldn't even have noticed.

But he took our work, apprentice poetry though it was, as seriously as he expected us to take our poetry. We were engaged in serious business, we had a chance to contribute to the great body of poetry that the world is in the continuous process of generating, and we were not going to waste that chance. That such insightful discussions could grow out of our poetry was amazing.

And he was honest. He told you straight, even when the news wasn't good. You found out quickly if you could take it. The ones who could were the ones who could get better. And if you couldn't take it, but you really wanted to write lasting poetry, you learned how to take it.

I remember especially the idea that what we were doing was *work*, and that we were learning a craft. That was good to know. Writing poetry wasn't some mysterious thing, though mystery is surely involved. Poetry wasn't something that magically came into being while we sat at our writing desks. We *made* those poems, and we were going to practice and practice that making and we were going to think about that making and we were going to talk about that making until our poems were as good as we could make them.

5

You could tell that he believed in poetry, believed that it could make a life, believed that it could *be* your life. You could see it in how hard he tried to help us understand why and how some of our poems were disasters, in how hard he wanted to teach us how to fix them. You could see it in the joy that he felt when one of our poems showed promise.

If one were to list all of the poets that came through his classes, here in Fresno and elsewhere, and then the students of those poets, one would see just how important Phil has been as a teacher. His influence will echo far into the future of American poetry.

He was a model. If you tried to be like him—if you took your craft as seriously as he did, if you took the work as seriously as he did, if you took your life as seriously as he did, if you believed in poetry in the way that he believed in poetry—then you had a chance to make work that could last.

Homage to Mr. Levine

KATHY FAGAN

Once a year or so, when I seem to forget myself and say something incisively critical about a student poem in class, bluntly, sometimes humorously; when I state with conviction what's "wrong" with a poem, or missing from it, or messy with it; when I joke about a bad move a poem has made, teasing it a little bit, acknowledging failure as quickly as success; I am not so much forgetting myself as remembering how I was taught to talk about poetry when I was young. I am lapsing back into the way my college classmates and I spoke to one another—the way Phil Levine spoke to us—as if we were, all twelve or fifteen of us, little Levines nearly every semester for three years. I realize now that it was like a private language, the kind some siblings develop. Once I entered grad school, I understood that my spoken comments—blessedly few, thanks to a natural shyness—were considered hard-ass. I was instructed to preface my remarks with phrases such as, "It seems to me that," and "If this were my poem I might," and "There is so much to admire here but I wonder just a bit about the . . ." Diplomacy didn't win me any new friends, but it didn't gain me new enemies either. And when I began to teach workshops of my own, as a blonde, blue-eyed, twenty-five-year-old doctoral student leading eighteen-year-old Mormons through the minefield that is Frank O'Hara, Sylvia Plath, and Langston Hughes, I was grateful to have had my poetry passion tempered. In those years, and all the years since then, I was reminded over and over that there is really only one of us who can get away with being Phil Levine, and it's not me.

In autumn 1977, I enrolled in Phil Levine's poetry workshop at Fresno State. I was beginning my sophomore year after a disastrous year as a scholarship student at a wealthy, Christian, Southern California college. I felt defeated, but my idea was to use up my California state tuition money for the year and then beat it out of Fresno, where my parents were living, as soon as I was able. I'd written poems at a nearby high school and knew about the legend that was Philip Levine. He lit student poems on fire with a cigarette lighter and stomped the flames out with his motorcycle boots. He cussed in the classroom. He was a card-carrying Communist. So the stories went. After the year I'd had battling fundamentalist right-wingers and Malibu millionaires, I thought, *Bring it, Levine.*

As it happened, there was no lighter, no motorcycle boots, no brandishing of membership cards. Phil, as he asked us to call him, had recently given up smoking and wore gym shoes every day. He was going to the gym. He complained about vision problems. He complained about almost everything. He laughed about almost everything, too. Or praised it: the perfection of the pear, the charm of the mockingbird—as if fruit or bird had just that morning come into being for him. He praised his wife's sense of humor, her cooking, her gardening skills. I had never heard a married person speak so fondly of his or her spouse, and that alone made Phil exotic to me.

Even after he had published more than five books and won a couple of significant national literary awards, Fresno State assigned Phil the requisite faculty load of composition courses. He walked to our class from one of them, stopping to pick up his mail on the way. Phil sat at a lab table–with–sink in front of the chalkboard—poetry workshops were held in one of the agriculture buildings—and flipped through his mail as students shuffled in, raising an eyebrow to a thin new volume of poems or wisecracking about a big poetry paycheck. He might read short passages to us from the books he was teaching in comp—Studs Terkel's *Working*, for example—before moving on to our work, chosen and mimeographed by him, two to five purple poems to a page. Often the odor of cow dung hung in the air, laced with the scent of gardenia on the best of days, pesticide on the worst. It was always either too hot or too foggy. An inversion could mean no blue sky for days, even weeks. In those days, Fresno State students were preppies in Izod, Ag kids in cowboy boots, or Bulldog fans in ball caps, but few of these enrolled in poetry workshop. It's possible I've conflated two or three workshops in my memory, but I know I capture the spirit of most of them when I say they consisted of a handful of badly dressed white kids like me, one or two Latino kids, a couple of war veterans, a girl who rode a Harley, and two or three older, nontraditional students with full-time jobs and families. The glory days of Larry Levis and David St. John, Roberta Spear, Lawson Inada, Gary Soto, Sherley Anne Williams, Sam Pereira, and other notables were long gone, and we newbies were irremediable dopes. But their legacy was palpable—perhaps because of the overt pride and pleasure Phil took in their successes—and I remember thinking of them as the older brothers and sisters who'd learned well, worked hard, and gotten the hell out of Fresno. Years later, when Larry Levis was my teacher at the University of Utah, I felt we indeed shared a psychic familial shorthand. Like Phil, Larry wore his intellect lightly. Like Phil, his devotion to the craft was infectious.

In the late 1970s, Phil's career was coming into full bloom. Stephen Yenser published an insightful and influential essay on Phil's work in *Parnassus* in 1977, before Levine turned fifty. It is remarkable to consider that he had already written his poems "Belle Isle, 1949," "On the Edge," "Animals Are Passing from Our Lives," "Heaven," the widely anthologized "To a Child Trapped in a Barbershop," the singularly spectacular "They Feed They Lion," and the disturbing "Angel Butcher." He was head-hunted to teach elsewhere. Spring semester '78 he went east to Tufts; someone named Mark Strand took his place at Fresno State. In three years Phil would leave Fresno again to teach at Columbia University, where I was a beginning MFA student. If it hadn't been for Phil, I wouldn't have been there. I remember distinctly, in 1979, looking up what the acronym MFA meant. I discussed programs with Phil, by which I mean he told me what three schools to apply to. I did as he said and got into all of them. A few months before I graduated with my BA in English, Mr. Levine, as I called him then—I was such a nitwit—Mr. Levine told me there were three things I'd need to be a poet: talent, perseverance, and luck. "You've got the talent," he said. "Only you can tell whether or not you've got the perseverance," he said. "And I'm your luck." The talent and luck parts sounded good to me. And though I thought I understood about perseverance at the time, I had no idea.

Phil often said to us in class that we had more interesting things in our pockets than in our poems. And he was right. That lint, loose tobacco, and couple of cents were infinitely more interesting than anything in our poems, and more useful. A similarly effective pedagogical method was to shake our poems above his desk—the lab table—and listen for the "real stuff," the good stuff, for *any* stuff to fall out of them. These were the best lessons in the value of concrete language and the importance of specificity, image, and detail to poetry that I've ever learned, and I use them with my own students and, secretly but without fail, on my own poems to this day. He also used baseball metaphors in class. One student was batting 200 with his poem one day, another student 300: "But you know what that means, don't you? You write one more hit and your batting average goes up to 400 and you sign a million dollar contract."

Eager to "stuff" my poems and improve my batting average, I submitted to workshop one semester a serial poem based on the immigration experiences of my Irish grandparents. After discussing two or three in the series, Phil urged me to title the poem. I said I was considering, "The Irish in America." Phil said, "Who are you, James Michener?" We laughed. Even I had heard of James Michener. "Very ambitious, very ambitious work." The poem was awful, of course, but I wrote poems off the energy of that single comment, "Ambitious," for years.

In those days it was true for the majority of Phil's Fresno State students that Poetry lived on the East Coast, if not in England, and we lived on the not-quite-West Coast. Crappy luck. Except Levine lived among us, too. He'd lived among those like us in Detroit. He continued to live in Detroit in his poems and continued to live in Fresno in real life. By choice. We were delighted when he complained about his "private school" students after returning from one of his East Coast teaching gigs. I'm not making too much of this when I claim that what Phil's work in the classroom and on the page did was stir our spirits out from under the crush and devastation of the ordinary, ugly, and poor, and because of that, poetry became possible for us. Because of Phil's subject matter, his prosody, his humor, his anger, his allegiances to and alliances with the political and social underclass, his students not only found a way to speak, but were reassured of their right to. The courage and confidence we'd been in danger of losing—to observe the world, criticize it, mourn it, praise it, analyze it, create and re-create it—were restored. And it became clear that if we chose to, and worked very hard, we might just make poets of ourselves, as Phil Levine had. Literature that had once seemed largely inaccessible or irrelevant to me and to my peers suddenly seemed necessary—ours for the taking and, most astonishingly, ours to make.

One story about Phil that I've doled out to only my nearest and dearest over the years happened while I was his student at Columbia in 1981. Phil was then the age that I am now. I honestly don't know how strange it was for him to be teaching at an Ivy League school, but for me, to be living in the dormitory that my grandmother had once cleaned at one of the most prestigious universities in the world made me both wildly happy and incredibly nervous, as if I could be found out and kicked out at any moment. Phil's appearance that year provided me with a touchstone, a sort of footing, though he treated us all the same and behaved in the classroom exactly as he had in Fresno. A poem once came up for workshop with the phrase "*habla español?*" Bizarrely, I'd managed to pick up no Spanish, either in New York where I'd been raised, or in California where I'd finished high school and gone to college. "What does that mean," I asked, "habla español?" "Do you speak Spanish," Phil answered. "No," I said, "that's why I'm asking." Phil dropped his head down on the workshop table and laughed. As if I had made an absurd and deliberate joke, which I hadn't. When I realized my gaffe, I suffered a moment of panic. I had exposed my ignorance, my inexperience, and an apparent ability to flaunt both.

I was not, after all, thrown out of the hallowed halls of Columbia University. Nevertheless, when I was finally willing to tell the *habla español* story, I told it for many years wincingly and with embarrassment. We are all of us breakable, but the unformed thing is especially fragile. There is a tenderness to most young people. I am gentle with my students because Mr. Levine was, in every essential way, gentle with me; I attend to their poems with seriousness because Mr. Levine attended to mine with seriousness. Writing of his teacher, John Berryman, Phil comments on Berryman's ability to "devastate the students' poems without crushing the students' spirits." Alas, there is no poet or teacher good enough to teach someone how to survive a life, much less a life of poetry. But Mr. Levine comes close. There is only one Phil Levine: just my luck.

Terrific

ANDREW FELD

In my private, Sei Shōnagon–like list of "Things That Make You Pleased To Be Alive" you'll find, somewhere near the top, "Phil Levine saying the word *terrific*."

"Clare's just terrific!" "Isn't that a terrific poem?" In a quick conversation under the deadening fluorescence of the AWP Bookfair, over the phone at a faculty prereading dinner (and how many of these, with strangers, semi-strangers, almost-friends, and the occasional true friend and fellow poet has Philip Levine had to endure in the course of his public career?), suddenly and gratifyingly bringing to a halt the menu and/or travel discussion: the mention of a poem, a book, a particular poet, and suddenly Phil swings forward, alive, alight. "Oh, she's a terrific poet!"

"Terrific" covers a lot of ground with Phil. When he says it, you still can see, just underneath the adult mask he wears with the prop moustache, the thirteen- or fourteen-year-old boy he once was, amazed with the music of poetic speech, or the slightly older boy in Mrs. Paperno's class, reading Wilfred Owen and realizing how poetry can serve "as an amulet against the lies that could deceive and undo me." This serious belief in the purpose and importance of poetry, along with a constant astonishment that such a thing can and does exist—the genuine—that poem, that poet, that book—what a pleasure! Isn't it just terrific?—this seems to me an intrinsic part of Phil Levine's particular brilliance, a vital aspect of his being-in-the-world. Under and along with all his serious scholarship and intellect, the deep study of the art and its history, the lifetime's work and the lifetime's accomplishment—which places him as one of the best poets of his generation (that astonishing generation of A. R. Ammons, Robert Creeley, Allen Ginsburg, James Merrill, Frank O'Hara, John Ashbery, W. S. Merwin, Adrienne Rich, and so many others)—the thrill, the energy that first drew him to poetry has in no way diminished. Mention a poem by Federico García Lorca, Rich, Michael Palmer, or the most recent book by one of the many poets drawn into his orbit, and there it is: the sheer pleasure in the art, the thrill: "Gee, what a terrific book that is!"

I have in my files a letter from Phil that I've thought about framing, because in it he says that a poem I had recently written is "a terrific poem." (I know: private correspondence/public usage—I'm sorry, Phil.) Every time I open the yellow, blue-lined piece of paper with his neat, semicursive/semiscript handwriting, I feel again the pleasure of receiving his praise. Especially because when I was actually in his workshop, at the University of Houston a few years before the letter, in the fall of 1997, Phil didn't seem to regard me as particularly terrific, although I think he did gradually warm to me. The word he first used—*twice*—to describe me (for the record: Phil has denied this, but I remember. I remember. And besides, I have witnesses) was *snob*. In retrospect, perhaps I shouldn't have come to class in a velvet smoking jacket and ascot. At least that's how I felt I was attired under the weight of his rebuke. The occasion was a poem I'd written about finding a page torn out of a porn magazine in the street—or that was the surface subject of the poem. The real subject was a virulent break-up I was going through at the time, and a certain amount of rage about that experience. None of which mattered at all to Phil—not the elaborate description of the woman, not my neat, rhymed and metered stanzas, not even all my Beckett quotes. My anger, he said, was misplaced. The woman in the pictures was the victim: she was being exploited. My anger should be directed at the man holding the camera—and even he was probably just some poor schmo toiling in the industry. Really, my anger should be directed at the real pimps who were profiting from this sorry business, the publishers, the guys in the higher offices, not the girl stripping naked for a few bucks.

This may seem like an obvious lesson in Phil Levine's view of the world (sympathy/empathy for the worker, rage against the system, etc.), the humanist value of seeing the particular (this girl, what particular forces conspired to force her into this particular form of subjection), and the old dictum that human beings, in the world and in poetry, should never be viewed as a means to an end. The answer is: it was all that, which is what made it so important and so completely different from all of my previous experiences in poetry workshops. First of all, there was the whole business of subject matter, which Phil directly attacked, along with the ethical, moral, and political implications of the subject matter. What kind of workshop leader addressed the "about" of a poem, and not the "how"? The way Phil brushed aside, went immediately past the "craft" of the poem (the implication—you're a poet: of course you have some skill in arranging language, it's nothing to pat yourself on the back about—was also liberating) to engage with the subject enough to be affronted by it, and then gave me his real-world reaction to the poem and the poet: all of this demonstrated the kind of honesty that I have come to believe is the primary requirement of a teacher.

During the class itself the lesson might not have been the most fun I'd ever had in a workshop, but once I had gotten over my defensive reaction/petulance, I realized that what my poem had received was the complete attention of Philip Levine. He hadn't treated me like a student or my poem like a student poem. If my work couldn't stand up to this kind of attention, then I'd better start writing better poems. In the succeeding weeks that workshop became the most fun, the most alive experience I'd ever had, I've ever had, in a classroom.

In my memory of that workshop, there seems to have been a kind of three-tier system in place, although the system and the tiers changed and shifted according to the poems up for consideration that day and the flexible dynamics of the workshop. Still, I think the idea of three separate, identifiable levels can be maintained, as long as levels aren't seen as hierarchical (there was no "star student" in the workshop: there was us, the MFA and PhD students, and there was Phil Levine: compared with the gulf between us and Phil, any differences between the students evaporated). On one level there were the students in their first year at Houston, some in their first graduate workshop and just starting the difficult business of figuring out what kind of poetry they wanted to write. With these students Phil was tremendously encouraging and, for want of a better word, instructive. He also seemed to have some kind of a magic gift for understanding which of the students in the room could be counted on to provide useful insight into another student's poem. When Phil called on you, you always felt there was a clear reason why you, out of all the people in the room, had been called. Maybe he read our files. Most likely, he just read us.

Lost in a kind of purgatorial middle tier were the students who had some degree, perhaps, of accomplishment, but who were writing poems that Phil just didn't like or couldn't entirely see the point of. Almost always, these were poems in which the poet, in an attempt at a then-voguish kind of experimentalism, employed deliberate emotional and narrative obscurity (I wrote one or two of these. I was not alone). Obscurity is, of course, not the same thing as difficulty, which is intrinsic to certain subjects and styles and is an aspect of many of the poets Phil Levine loves. As the tedious discussion of "Why Is Poetry Difficult?" is on everyone's list of "Discussions That Bore One to Sleep," I'll stop here. When Phil encountered a poem that seemed deliberately obscure, and seemed to intentionally exclude the reader, he entertained us with stories about his time in Spain and Detroit. Phil's mind is never tedious. This was another lesson.

On the last tier were the students who were near the end of their MFA or PhD slog and were, for better or worse, fairly well along the identifiable path of their aesthetic: which is to say that some of us were, in that workshop, writing poems that would be included in our first books. (Only one of my poems from that workshop made it to my first book: "They Have a Name For It." Phil thought the line "At this point I would like to state my solidarity with the working classes" was hilarious, even though I'd written it as a kind of friendly jibe. More importantly, for me, he praised the poem by recognizing its debt to Cesare Pavese, whose work I'd been reading, in the William Arrowsmith translation, on Phil's very strong recommendation.)

Phil praised us and shared his excitement at our progress, but then he'd bring alive for us in the room the power of a Lorca poem. "You know what's really depressing?" a student said in the hallway during workshop intermission. "I'm already older than Lorca and I haven't written a poem that good." "You will never write a poem as great as Lorca," Phil said in a kind of instant response, and then, more gently, "none of us will." We all understood and appreciated the gesture of inclusion in that "us," and even more the clear, if terrifying, standards Phil Levine held, and that they did not, do not, vary according to which room he finds himself in. *Terrifying* is, after all, a word that, for all the difference in usage, means pretty much the same thing as *terrific*.

A Light Inside

NICK FLYNN

I think about Phil Levine nearly every day, whenever I sit down to write. He said something to me once—I assume he wouldn't remember, and if he did he wouldn't know the long-lasting effects his words had on me—but these few words set me—my life, my writing—off in another direction than the one in which I was headed. I'd handed in a poem for our one workshop together (at New York University)—I don't recall which poem, or whether it ever even became a poem—and after Phil read it he turned to me and said, *You've got more light inside you than this.*

By the time I made it to NYU I'd been out of school for a long time (ten years or so), working at various jobs (*lousy jobs* as Phil would say about his own jobs in his twenties, though I suspect neither of us found them completely, or merely, lousy). I'd been an electrician, an okay carpenter, a ship's captain (with a bona fide marine merchant's license), a caseworker with homeless adults. I liked the jobs, and if I didn't I made it clear and was fired—every restaurant I ever worked in fired me. My mother had worked in restaurants my entire life, after working at her truly lousy bank job all day. She worked nights at bars or restaurants for the tips, and we lived off her tips—she drilled it into my brother and me that if we didn't have enough to tip well, we didn't have enough to go out (which meant I almost never went out, except to bars, until I was thirty). During my ill-fated attempts at restaurant work, if customers were surly or rude to me I'd go into a silent rage, or if they tipped poorly I'd chase them into the parking lot and throw the money at them—clearly sublimated and misdirected defenses of my mother and what she must have endured, all those years.

That I can write about this now is thanks to Phil Levine—his poems gave all of us permission to write about the actual, day-in-day-out circumstances of our lives. That I can actually look someone in the eye and call myself a poet is thanks to Phil Levine. He made what seemed an unlikely path seem noble. His definition of a poet, I once heard him say (on the radio? in an essay? from a stage? to my face?) was someone who can look you in the eye—I took this to mean something about integrity, something about doing the best you could do. It was not simply a calling, which might suggest a lack of agency—it was something you had to become, to rise to, to embody. It would require everything. He once said (in an interview? in our workshop?) that being a poet is the one job in the world where you wake up every morning and nothing you know will help you to approach the task at hand, which is to write a poem. If you had remained an electrician, you would know how to get the lights to come on, but you are now a poet, and each day you must invent the world. Not the world, but your place in it. In this Phil is similar to another poet whom I also think about nearly every day, each time I find myself in another poem: Stanley Kunitz said that if you read a poem you like, you must become the person who can write that poem. It is a life's work. How one lives one's life is important. These are things Phil Levine has said to me, over the years, or that he has written in essays, or that I culled from his poems—it all blurs together now.

In 1992—twenty years ago now—I met Phil Levine in that workshop. It was my second year at NYU. When I first got there I was hungry to sit around a table and listen to real poets talk about poems. I saw it as another apprenticeship, not much different from the one I'd gone through to become an electrician. I was writing like a fiend, in a glorious fever—grateful that I'd escaped the burning house of my twenties (or so I believed). I'd already studied with great poets at NYU (Sharon Olds, Galway Kinnell, William Matthews), but I knew Phil was coming, and he was the reason I was there, though I didn't know it at that point, not fully. You see, I was, and likely still am, a blunt tool, a dull instrument. I need poems drilled into me, I needed to be strapped to a chair. At NYU Sharon had welcomed me into the community of poets and instilled the sense of poetry as a gift (I believe she even quoted from Lewis Hyde's *The Gift*). Galway recited Yeats and we'd all go on retreats, the entire class, into the woods, to write. At NYU I got to study with Ginsberg, who cried when he talked about Kerouac and who hit on me—he hit on everyone. But my last semester Phil was coming, we all knew he was coming (like Grendel), and we knew he would kick some ass. Phil made me want to show up each week and make him pay attention, if only because he didn't let a lazy word or phrase slip past. Anything that was false, or untransformed, or tired, he simply skipped over—he wouldn't waste his, or anyone else's, time. He was exactly what I needed.

I already knew him from his poems, everyone did. *What Work Is* had just come out (I think of it as his *Some Girls*—a masterpiece coming years after his early fury, especially [for me] *They Feed They Lion*). His poems did what I hoped mine would one day do, not only in their seeming effortlessness, but in their unlikely vistas, opening. At some point I read his essay on John Berryman—I identified with him sneaking into Berryman's Iowa workshop, unregistered, with his pride at getting over. I identified with his hunger to learn, after those years of lousy jobs. I identified with the fact that he stuck it out. He found a poet that was his (Keats), just as Kinnell had Yeats, and Olds found Lucille Clifton, and Ginsberg found Blake, and Kunitz found Celan. One line from his Berryman essay stayed with me (this is from memory)—"A poet does not play fast and loose with the facts of this world." Phil attributes this to Berryman, but what could it mean? Berryman, after all, had poems with talking sheep in them (*I hope the barker comes*). Look back at the title poem from *They Feed They Lion*:

> Out of burlap sacks, out of bearing butter,
> Out of black beans and wet slate bread . . .

This is Phil both wrestling with the facts of this world (auto plants, race riots) and simultaneously pulsing deeply into its unseen music . . .

> From my five arms and all my hands,
> From all my white sins forgiven, they feed . . .

A poet's job is not to play fast and loose with the facts of this world. What this would come to mean to me is that there is a world, one that demands—requires, rewards—our attention to it, the type of attention Simone Weil describes as prayer. The world is made up of hidden patterns, as-yet undiscovered physical properties, and it is our job to both honor these patterns and to invent new ones. To imagine. Berryman's sheep say what sheep would say, as far as we can imagine, if we are able to listen.

I cannot claim Phil Levine as my teacher alone—he belongs to many, most notably, and poignantly, Larry Levis, who died young a few years after I met Phil. Phil's love of Levis was manifest, and generous, and profound. His reputation as a hard-ass followed him, and was deserved, yet it made his generosity that much more genuine. In workshop, I happened to find myself on his good side, or at least that's how I remember it. If he humiliated me, or my poems, I don't remember. He was committed to the poem; we were being offered the chance to be part of a long tradition, stretching back centuries; we were being invited to gaze into that river with him, to be a part of it.

The poems I was writing then were dark, gloomy (some might say I still am). Phil turned to me one day, during our weekly workshop, and said that he didn't believe the poem I'd handed in. "You've got more light inside you than this," he told me, looking me straight in the eye. His words pierced me—it was as if someone had really seen me, had acknowledged who I was, had pulled aside my mask of gloom. He did not use the word *luminous*—this is not a word I would associate with Phil—it's not demotic enough, not of this earth. I knew I had light inside me, and that somehow I would have to find a way to let some of it into my poems. It would take me years, but Phil's voice stayed with me, along with his faith that there was more than darkness inside me, inside any of us. He had seen it (at least he said he had), years before I could.

Thirty Years from Somewhere

EDWARD HIRSCH

Detroit, 1982. I was thirty-two, had just published my first book, and was teaching at Philip Levine's alma mater, Wayne State University, which, as he once said, "wasn't trying to be the Harvard of Shitville, it was just trying to be what it was," a concrete campus for commuters, a school for the city. His twin brother, Eddie, a painter who ran a business buying and selling parts for heavy vehicles, invited me over for brunch to meet Phil and Franny.

Phil was fifty-four at the time. He had published ten books. He was for me the model of an urban poet. I had been overwhelmed by his ferocious books of rage, *Not This Pig* and *They Feed They Lion*, the moving elegies of *1933*, the vanished utopia and anarchist dream of *The Names of the Lost*. His poems were as tough as the cities he celebrated—Detroit, Fresno, Barcelona. I was in awe. I was so nervous and agitated to meet a poet who already mattered so much to me that I sweated through my shirt on the drive over to Royal Oak.

Eddie opened the door and I did a double take—he was a heavier version of Phil, who was then instantly recognizable to me, partly because I had seen his photograph in a couple of anthologies, partly because I had been reading him since I was a teenager. Some poets surprise you when you meet them—they don't seem like the authors of their own work—but Phil looked the way he was supposed to look. He fit his poems. He was taut and wiry, like a lightweight boxer who had kept his fighting shape. He hit the gym regularly. He looked like he could still get in trouble in a bar. He was youthfully middle aged—relaxed, alert. His eyes were clear, kind, steely. He had thick hair, long sideburns, and sported a bushy mustache, like Burt Reynolds in *Smokey and the Bandit*. He laughed deeply and had what my parents called "Depression teeth." I noticed his unusually long and tapered hands. He was handsome in a slightly off-kilter way.

That day Phil greeted me in his brother's house, a familial setting, and I warmed to him right away. He was then as he is now—unnervingly direct, outrageously funny. He had a blue-collar mode, which I recognized from my hometown of Chicago. He was a plainspoken, no-bullshit urban intellectual, like one of our favorite figures, Studs Terkel. He stood his ground and told you what he thought. He had a brother with the same deep voice—when they talked it came at you in stereo—and a wife who matched him, too, a softer presence, a sweetening influence, a no-holds-barred beauty.

I was initiated into the Levine world. He lived up to his poems. He believed in the dignity of ordinary people, working people. He was loyal to his past. He had worked in factories in the forties and fifties—the injustices still rankled him. It was as if he had just gotten out of there. He had a special animus for General Motors. He seemed to consider Henry Ford a personal enemy. He didn't like bosses, factory apparatchiks, English department chairs, university deans. He didn't like whiners and crybabies, pretentious assholes, right-wing jerks. There were plenty of racists and anti-Semites around when he was growing up in Detroit—they still disgusted him. He never pulled a punch. He was allergic to lying. Poetry careerists simply annoyed him—he'd rather talk about the pleasures of red wine or the sweet science of boxing.

There was a moment when Phil went to the john. Eddie and I were talking about a couple of mutual friends in Detroit. I mentioned a poet we both knew well. "He's the angriest man I've ever met," I said.

"You didn't know my brother in his heyday," Eddie replied.

It was true. By all accounts, I encountered a mellower version of Phil Levine. Knuckleheads still pissed him off, but he no longer got into fistfights. He just turned his back on strivers and creeps. The old fires still burned, but by the time I knew him Phil's rage had been tempered by grief, success, and age. He was seeking a greater range of tones. He had decided to become a poet of joy as well as of suffering. He had entered his middle period and gotten as far as the celebratory lyrics, the dark optimism, of *Seven Years from Somewhere* and *One for the Rose*.

It didn't take me long to learn that Philip Levine read poetry with his pulse and believed in working hard. He still aspired to be the great poet of Detroit. He aligned himself with the poets of the Spanish Civil War—Raphael Alberti, Federico García Lorca, Miguel Hernández. He embraced the odes of Pablo Neruda, the *poemas humanos* of César Vallejo. He loved the poetry of his former student Larry Levis, his good friend Galway Kinnell, his beloved teacher John Berryman. He didn't like the pretentiousness of his teachers Robert Lowell (Iowa) and Yvor Winters (Stanford). He could still appreciate their poems, but he mocked their classroom styles. He admired the hell out of the poetry of his classmates—Peter Everwine, Donald Justice, Thom Gunn. He could do a dead-on imitation of the Polish poets Czeslaw Milosz and Zbigniew Herbert. He knew stone cold the lyrics of the Elizabethans, the fragments of the modernists. He had an ear for jazz, a gift for narrative. He was a romantic in the American grain, John Keats by way of William Carlos Williams, Walt Whitman filtered through Dylan Thomas and Hart Crane. He still believed in the boundlessness of the human. His attitude toward poetry was all or nothing. He was all in.

That day we started talking about poetry and our friendship began. The next visit we drove through northwest Detroit. We drove along Grand Boulevard and passed through miles and miles of empty lots, abandoned buildings, wasted places. The city had never recovered from the violence of 1967. We drove out to the old Ford River Rouge Complex in Dearborn. It was enormous, like the past, which needed to be saved, since so much had been torn down and lost. We drove along the river, the factories spouting fire, and drank it all in.

After that trip to Detroit, Phil and I started exchanging letters and talking everywhere. I've always loved his anecdotes and stories, his fiery take on life, its puzzles and enigmas, its deep mysteries. We started to pore over each other's poems. I learned quickly never to ask his opinion if I didn't really want an honest answer. He's ruthlessly truthful. I came to rely on his forthrightness. I've never known him to duck a question. Over the years, I've talked to him about everything that has mattered to me. Sometimes he has been more like an older brother, or a father.

I can close my eyes and see us talking about poetry at conferences and festivals, in public and private, in down-home gyms and hotel workout rooms, over hundreds of suppers, most of them cooked by Franny. I see us

71

chattering across the tennis court; we're batting it back and forth in Fresno and Somerville, at the Bread Loaf Writers' Conference; we're hammering it out in Santa Monica and East Lansing, in Krakow and Prague, Houston and Brooklyn; we're crossing the country with it; it's carrying us from Los Angeles to New York. I've learned so much from that conversation, our friendship, which has endured for thirty years and deepened into one of the graces of my life.

Philip Levine

The Proof of My Patience

SANDRA HOBEN

"Send me some poems," he said.

It must have been 1972, the Squaw Valley Community of Writers. Phil had read for scholarships, and I received one. And of course Phil took the time to send a letter to Edith Jenkins, the teacher at Oakland's Grove Street Community College who'd written me a reference. "You must be a poet," Phil wrote to Edith, "because your students are writing so well."

I recall little about what went on in the workshops at Squaw. I don't recall Phil praising my work, or blasting it. What I do remember was the conference I had with him.

I remember the rather crappy cafe at ground level where I was waiting for Phil to show up for our conference. It was summer, but the sky opened up and lightning struck all over the mountain. David Perlman, science editor of the *San Francisco Chronicle*, stood with me, watching the bolts, the downpour. "This doesn't happen," he said, "in the Sierra in summer." Then he counted the seconds; I learned something new about the distance between lightning and thunder. And I was about to learn something else: that Philip Levine would become my teacher, my mentor, my friend.

Phil finally arrived at the cafe. Again, I don't recall that we went over any of my poems. We talked. We drank coffee that tasted like pencil shavings. "There are three students here that are writing well," he said, "and you are one of them. I'm never coming back here," he said. And he never did.

"Send me some poems," he said, and gave me his address. For a year we corresponded; we got into a groove. Each month I would mail off three poems, and he would reply with a letter on yellow legal paper, written with a good pen; and he'd mark up my poems and comment on them. It was a wonderful year. I had him to myself once a month. And of course I had taken to writing on yellow legal pads, and had obtained an expensive fountain pen, a Parker 61, the one that inks by osmosis. I couldn't afford such a pen, but I found it at the UC Berkeley bowling alley. The pen just sat there, in a lovely wooden groove, where a writing instrument could rest. Is any of this true? Did UC Berkeley even *have* a bowling alley? What was I doing, who was I with? But I kept the Parker: it was a sign. No. Somebody left a pen behind, and I slipped it into my bag. Yellow pads and expensive pens: that was going to do the trick. Poetry turned out to be a lot more than paper and pen: the art of poetry would be work, hard work, and would take a long time, and a lot of failure.

And the letters themselves, well, that's another story.

Sometime in the spring of '73, I made my decision: I would move to Fresno for an MA in English, with an emphasis in creative writing. I had a BA from St. John's College, a lot of science, math, philosophy, and some literature dressed up like philosophy. No creativity in that scene. I had moved to Berkeley and was grateful to have had Edith Jenkins and the Grove Street Community College.

When I left Berkeley, I lost my community of friends, the original Peet's coffee shop, I lost the fog and the breeze, the used book stores, and the trips to Shell Beach.

I was lonely in Fresno that first semester and couldn't write a decent poem for months. My poems were like roadkill, nothing to resuscitate. Couldn't I go back to my Berkeley house, my friends, the year of exclusive correspondence with Phil? Correspondence is one thing, a workshop with Phil and a hand-ful of talented students—that was a whole different deal. And Phil was not easy on me. I was somewhat buoyed up when a kid confided that Phil never praised him, or made fun of that student's work. I didn't say it, but I got it: this kid had no talent, and Phil was not going to shred a young person who'd never be a poet. I understood: Phil was hard on me because he believed in me.

One of Phil's ways of dealing with bad poems was to make you laugh, but when you got home things weren't very funny: my poem stinks. Then there was the evening everybody failed and turned in bad poems: "These poems are worse than a newspaper, and poems are supposed to last forever."

Sometime in that semester I walked into Phil's office and sat down. "I can't write anything." His response: "You must change your life." What I needed and what I would slowly receive was the friendship of my peers: Roberta Spear, Paul Saupe, Ernie Benck, Suzanne Lummis, Jon Veinberg, Ernesto Trejo.

Without noticing it, I'd written a poem. A found poem. Each day I wrote in my journal and would look over the week's work—and there was "Pennies." I didn't recall writing the piece, but it was in my journal and in my handwriting. I turned in the poem to the workshop, not expecting much of a response. Phil asked what the group had to say. And they went after me; after all, I'd been writing poorly: "She's using *it* too many times," or "too many repetitions of *here*." Then Phil had his say. He didn't say *terrific*, he didn't say *marvelous*, but he was clearly taken with the poem. He was delighted. An immature character had shown up in the last stanza, in the last lines:

> I could spit
> mouthfuls of pennies at him,
> but I know he'd spend them on himself
> and write,
> saying he'd fallen in love,
> saying *thank you*.

"Yes," Phil said, "he wrote to her, perhaps a postcard . . ."

The next two semesters of workshop were with Peter Everwine and Chuck Hanzlicek, during which I wrote poems, some of them good, and some had to be defenestrated. But I was writing, and both Chuck and Peter were wonderful teachers.

In the evening workshop, Phil was tough; in the afternoon's Spanish Poetry in Translation class, he had a different demeanor. Phil and José Elgorriaga cotaught the course. Elgorriaga, a native speaker and chair of the Foreign Language Department, helped us with our Spanish, the puns, the colloquialisms. Phil pushed the poems, turning them into American English. The word *genial* was used a lot in that class, maybe more so from Elgorriaga, but also from

Phil. And the stakes weren't as high—if you make an error in a translation, no big deal; you weren't facing your own poems, just bad translations. Phil was teaching the class, but he was also working on his own writing, translating the Gloria Fuertes book. His own creativity was in play—sometimes he'd just stare out the window at the afternoon light.

Once Roberta Spear arrived late (she had finished her master's but sat in on some classes; she didn't attend workshops, she'd found her own voice). When Roberta walked in, Phil looked up and said, "Hi, sweetheart," something he wouldn't say in a workshop. Or so I think.

In translation class, the most hilarious error was made by Roberta. She'd been working on a Gloria Fuertes poem—a street scene, a tough neighborhood, and its characters. Then she spoke the phrase "and Pepe plays golf." I thought Elgorriaga might fall off his chair: "Pepe plays golf? No! Pepe is a pimp!" But Roberta was certain she'd looked up the word. Check with me first, Elgorriaga said. It was easy to laugh at errors in translations. I can still hear her laughter.

Then the discussion about which poems are untranslatable. Phil said that "The Emperor of Ice Cream" could never be translated. Not possible.

Like my experience in workshop, I was slow on the mark for Spanish Poetry in Translation. I'd chosen the early work of Pablo Neruda—oh, the despair. I dragged in another Neruda poem based on a pun. If the poem isn't any good, then the translation can't fire. Then one day I brought in a Juan Ramón Jiménez poem, "Yellow Spring." It was about yellow and about spring. There was music in the piece, but I hadn't noticed. Phil looked up at me and said one word: *talent*.

I also took an individual study on rhyme and meter with Phil. Again, a slow start. My first piece was about dolphins communicating, something from the news, I suspect. "You don't care about this," he said. But then I succeeded. I don't recall the whole poem, but it started with, "Get up, let out the cat and stare / at children." I was writing about ordinary things in my life, and the rhymes, the off-rhymes, the meter worked well. "Where did you get this? Where is your time card?" he wanted to know.

I continued to correspond with Phil when I was at the University of Utah, and beyond. I finished the PhD but was soured by academia. Everwine warned me about going to Utah—"just get a job," the wise man said. But I didn't listen. After Utah, I just wanted a job, not a position. While I was finishing my dissertation, I worked as a paralegal in San Francisco, and I liked the action. I had personal knowledge of certain activities (a tweaked sentence, stolen from Didion). Then I had enough of that job.

Roberta Spear worked for a while as a social worker, and brought up a family; she continued to write. And Jon Veinberg had, well, just a job, while writing his poetry and other creative endeavors. There is a tradition of poets having a day job—Wallace Stevens at The Hartford, William Carlos Williams with his patients. Many of Phil's students went on to head creative writing programs and did terrific work. But some of us took other paths. Whatever the path, I had enduring friendships from the Fresno poetry community, and help with my writing, especially from Roberta Spear and Phil.

After I married and had a son, I settled in Mill Valley and taught at a college and as a poet-in-the-schools. My favorite students were first-graders, with their wonderful imaginations and their fearlessness. I returned to Fresno as often as I could; I'd meet with Roberta, Jean Janzen, and sometimes Dixie Salazar, and we'd go over our poems. Roberta was my first reader. She was an essential part of the Fresno poetry community; Phil made that statement in his letter to her, which she showed to me at the Stanford Medical Center. Her death, in 2003, was a devastating loss.

Sam Hamill, of Copper Canyon Press, suggested publishing the new and selected poems of Roberta Spear; Phil was to select the poems and write an introduction, which he did. Because Sam was no longer with Copper Canyon, we chose publisher Malcolm Margolis of Heyday Books. Phil, Peter, and I facilitated the publication of Roberta's *A Sweetness Rising: New and Selected Poems, Edited and with an Introduction by Philip Levine*. A terrific book, and again, there it is: Phil's generosity.

My friend Tilly Nylin, a visual artist, has a mantra: *go where the art is*. I'd noticed that there was a lot of activity around the 2010 Levis Symposium at the Virginia Commonwealth University, Phil the keynote speaker. *Go where the poetry is*. The symposium was a blast, old friends and new, a wonderful gathering, a celebration of Larry Levis's life and work, and of poetry itself. When I left, I reinvented the manuscript I'd fought with for forty years.

"You, Sandra," Phil once said, "are the proof of my patience."

Philip Levine has given me so much: he's given me laughter; he's spent his own creative energy helping me with my writing; he was there to slash the weeds and let the poem bloom, when no one else could. He believed in me. When I wrote to him, he always responded, with letters that ended with—

Love, Phil

An Exquisite Simulacrum

ISHION HUTCHINSON

In the foul rag-and-bone shop of the heart.
—W. B. YEATS

It was a late evening in the fall semester of 2007 when I first met Philip Levine.
New York University's Creative Writing Program had recently moved out of
the literature building on University Place, where the classrooms with their
long narrow tables and drab colors seemed to have been made for executive
board meetings, into a beautiful, labyrinthine apartment building called the
Lillian Vernon Creative Writers House on West Tenth Street and Sixth Avenue.
I had no quarrel with the move, except that now my two haunts, the main
library and Washington Square Park, were no longer next door; in fact, I was
in high spirits, buzzing with the other students sitting under the chandelier
about how suitable our new baroque classroom was for writing our magna
opera. But the buzz—oh the portraits, oh the stained-glass windows, oh the
carpets, oh the books—was a mask for what was truly ticking in our heads:
the impending arrival of Philip Levine. None of us, if I am recalling correctly,
had worked with him before, but we were not strangers to the mixed rumors
of his pedagogical approach—surgical, no anesthesia. We knew we were
waiting on someone important, to be owners of his myth, and we were all

open for something important to happen to us, a miracle of a kind, which was why, I suppose, when the great mensch opened the door, we all fell silent. He wore a light, faded jacket, unzipped to show a faded T-shirt, a peak cap, also faded, and carried a small dark bag in one hand. Paused on the top of the stairs, he looked, I thought, like a skinnier Clint Eastwood, squinting, I guess, because of the chandelier's glow. Before descending the three or four steps, he smiled, our breaths returned, the chandelier pulsed brighter over our heads, and when he creaked down into his chair at the head of the table, his presence closer, I had the sense that I was one of the twelve at the Last Supper. And so it was, for his opening remarks reminded us that this was his last class before retiring (he was eighty, after all), and as if to stem an outbreak of melancholy, wine (I am guessing it came from his bag, but where the cups emerged from, I have no idea) was served as we introduced ourselves. When my turn came to say my name, I did, and Phil said, "Eh?" So I repeated my name, louder, but he rose up out of his chair not a little bit perturbed, said "Ah shit," and walked out of the room. The chandelier exploded in my chest, trampled by wild horses, all the portraits knitted their brows, the other students looked at me, their eyes saying what was ringing in my head: what the hell did you do? Phil, who was out of the room for less than five minutes, aeons for us, returned and apologized for his sudden exit. He explained while sitting back down that he had a heart condition of some kind, so at times he had to coax back his heart to normal. Taking a sip from his Styrofoam cup, looking now at me—definitely Clint Eastwood—he asked for my name again. Now my heart was off-kilter, palpitating at a staggering rate. But somehow I managed to pronounce my name in a measured tone; he nodded, and thus, after almost giving each other heart attacks, we met.

The semester's diastole and systole unfolded many glorious moments. Phil's marvelous giving spirit extended beyond his role as teacher and he treated us like peers, members of the same tribe, despite our varying limitations as poets. Direct honesty, that was the outfit of the class; for us the unspoken code was no fences keep good poets. Through Phil's voice, as autumn deepened into winter, we got to the bone of what it means to live—and live long—in poetry. His stories were benedictions; they brought, to take a phrase from Donne, "a heart into the room." Listening to Phil, I was enthralled not only with the voice's cadence—a private laugh seems to lurk beneath his words even when he is at his most serious—but the exactness of details. It was superb the way he fixed recollections with not only dates and time, but season and

79

weather, which made all of his tales live, intimate, and fresh, leaving us with the impression that they were being told for the first time, and only to us. I loved to hear those stories so much that I was annoyed whenever we had to get back to a poem at hand. Often, watching him talk with his head cocked to one side, I saw the younger Phil's head on the other side, listening, riveted to this bespectacled sage.

Typically, a student would read his or her poem, after which the rest of us abused or complimented it according to our cardinal humors while Phil sat listening, doodling on a sheet of paper, waiting for our appraisal to end. It never failed to amaze me, after all the laps we had just run around the poem, the way Phil began his critique with seismographic precision: "You could at least get the grammar right—it is the first line," and we bowed our heads back to the page, the glaring error mooning us. After that he made other revelations, the poem—lucky bastard!—dwindled in stature, accelerated in possibility. Then a moment would come when he moved off the chart, to a memory. These reminiscences could be considered midrashic the way they distilled a poem by lifting it from the coffin of the page to a living past, Phil's, but—and extraordinarily—all of the literature that came before it, for Phil was a venerable repository of great literature. Phil's memory reminded us of the primitivity of poetry, and because he taught through telling, with the bare human voice, he took us back to a place where language was consecrated with one fire. (This is not to say Phil's language itself was "consecrated"—he once said something I repeat every chance I get, "Don't fuck with the muse." Here of course Phil was delighting in a nuanced take on Keats's claim that the poet is the most "unpoetical of all God's Creatures.") If we had closed our eyes—I did a couple of times—it would not have been hard to imagine the chandelier on the floor, stiff flames pointing up, and Phil, our tribe's elder in T-shirt and windbreaker, his voice sparkling from the bulbs, animating in us the long love he has carried for the old art. Without being preachy he made something burn in us, and we were willing neophytes, transfigured after each class. The classroom essentially became a veritable salon, one in which not just the living souls enjoyed the flame, but the dead came to warm themselves. Keats was spoken of as if he were making his way down Broadway to class. Edward Thomas entered with his notebooks and mud-caked shoes. Dylan Thomas poured the wine, Hopkins blessed it. Berryman shouted down the furnace at Blake (and at Shadrach, Meshach, and Abendego). Roethke exchanged whispers with Christopher Smart. When Phil spoke of Lorca, Machado, and

Neruda ("the pinnacle, the apex, the Alp" to quote what a Spanish tutor said about Machado to Phil once, recorded in Phil's brilliant essay "Living in Machado"), as much as I had read them before, I went home to read them again, and understood what Herbert meant by "the soul in paraphrase, heart in pilgrimage." It was in Phil's class that I came to realize there were other Italians besides Dante and Montale: Pavese soon shoveled his solitude into my head, and Quasimodo, who was still a cathedral bell-ringer, only with poems, and not hunchbacked, broke that solitude. (Many other Italians have since ensued.) Almost every week after leaving Phil's class I headed to the library, my trek slightly longer, to find whatever book he had mentioned in class. So many and diverse were they that I am certain I have been to every floor of that immense library. There was something validating and exhilarating when I finished reading a line of his recommendation and heard his sprite whispering somewhere in the air, "Isn't that marvelous?" The heart murmured, yes. Even now, years after, the heart is murmuring yes.

That semester I was on a pilgrimage for my own kind of tune to fit the vision I had left home, Jamaica, with; but having been in New York City for more than a year, I felt the vision going soft. The first time I brought a poem to class, Phil put it properly in its place: "Too grandiose." Another time: "Crane," he said, "not easy to do." How exact, for at the time I was worshipping at the church of Crane and Merrill. I pitched to something else. Though there was no praise, I detected that Phil saw I wasn't wasting his time, and he said incredibly encouraging things to me, inside and outside of class. I had something of an epiphany one day when he said to me, "You know, Ishion, humor is one of the great universal conditions your work could benefit from," or some such piece of wisdom. Suddenly, forgotten phrases from Henri Bergson's essay on laughter, which I had studied and loved in college, geysered up in my mind—"laughter always implies a kind of secret freemasonry, or even complicity." (Incidentally, the previous year I had received a letter from an old lady in Jamaica imploring me to put "more smiles" in my poetry after she read a poem of mine in a local paper. Clearly I had not made any progress.) Diligently, sleeplessly, I worked to better my tone, and toward the end of the semester, the city darker and colder, I felt something freshen in the lines. *Merci*, Phil, for what you aerated. The only way young poets can express their gratitude to a master is to continue in greater intensity their apprenticeship, so three years after that class, I mailed my first book, *Far District*, to him. I remember my accompanying note was a longish apology; I didn't want to provoke another heart condition. When I got Phil's letter, handwritten on a yellow legal pad, my heartbeats pulverized the deserts of Utah, where I was hermitting away in Salt Lake City. Holding the letter was like holding warm glass, a bulb from our chandelier; I held tightly and read myself into a sort of lachrymal deficiency. Remembering the letter now I still experience a small threat of the deficiency, not because of the tremendous kindness Phil showed in it, but because the U.S. Postal Service lost the letter several months later, along with some of my most treasured possessions. On one of the numerous occasions I had to describe to a postal agent the contents of the missing boxes, I wailed: "There is a letter from Phil, Philip Levine, in an envelope in a tan notebook. I need it." The exasperation of both of us clogged the receiver.

The last time I saw Phil at NYU was at my graduate reading wine reception held at the Creative Writers House; the reading itself took place in one of the colossal halls near the library. On that occasion, two of my very good friends, the gifted poets Adam Wiedewitsch and Dante Micheaux, and I decided to attend dapperly dressed in matching outfits, emulating, I supposed the Rat Pack. There was no shortage of compliments from everyone about our black vests and black ties and long-sleeved white shirts; we moved singularly, a Hydra amid the wine drinkers in the room. Then we saw Phil, back turned to us, commanding a group. He must have sensed us and turned sharply around: "Hey, Dante, Ishion, Adam," a pause, then the scalpel, "what are you guys, waiters?" All eyes were on us, laughter charged the room. No doubt, humor is one of the great human conditions, and so is humility, which I feel always for knowing Philip Levine. To end, since I have made something both imagined and recalled, please, Marvell, raise my apologia:

Pardon me, *Mighty Poet*, nor despise
My causeless, yet not impious, surmise.

The Surprising Chill

LAWSON FUSAO INADA

The entire line was, is—"The surprising chill of a September morn"—by poet Carol Howard. But it was recited by the teacher, several times—with the grace and gestures of a conductor—before he wrote it on the board in his elegant script. Ah, yes—the flow . . .

And there we were in a clunky Cold War complex on the steppes—but in a classroom with the air of a conservatory, where the teacher regarded us with warmth, respect. As poets.

Thus, even the conventional textbook took on a transformative aura, and even though an Emily Dickinson, for instance, could be dispensed with in short order, as an "assignment," she was a tall order for her fellow poets who hunched over her in library recesses, cloistered, mouths moving to her music. And mystery. How did she do it?

Evenings, while I tended to a plot of words, my father, a former fieldworker, would intone passages of poetry, over and over, varying pauses, being trained in *shigin*—traditional, songlike recitation—which, upon approval of the teacher, could lead to being called upon to preside at ceremonial occasions. It was a calling; still, poetry was poetry, and it all fit.

Our teacher, our sensei, was also a master of recitation, and with an uncanny immediacy, urgency, could project, transport us to a "contagious hospital" in

New Jersey, and then we'd be in a "flee from me" location in olde England. Poetry is poetry . . .

Meanwhile, we huddled masses had miles to go, since so much depends on a jar in Tennessee, and my initial attempt at "verse"—unlike my scribblings, sprawlings in a tablet—was laboriously typed, clunked out on my mother's college machine. The "verse" began—"What sort of man was Charlie Parker, who"—and thus began a further relationship with the teacher, who had "heard the Bird" in Detroit. The Bard! Wonder of wonders—in the English Department—which coincided with the fact that, several months earlier, on a meandering sojourn at Cal, I had managed to matriculate under the tutelage of, not only "The Pres," but the Muse herself—"Lady Day"! In order to "woodshed," I returned home.

We took it from there, listening sessions—private "bom-Bard-ments"—in our respective homes; but as for his own "blowing," all I knew was that he was "writing poetry," so I assumed he was "woodshedding" also. Then, too, as a new teacher, and young at that, his only distinction was that he taught "elective" classes.

However, when asked, he did mention some recent appearances in publications not available in the campus library—the "periodicals" alcove akin to a walk-in closet. This was, after all, a former normal school where parking was a priority. Ah, but the teacher, always generous, loaned me his personal copies.

What a revelation! A "surprising chill"! Formidable verse! The teacher could really "blow"! His poetry could have readily graced, enhanced, expanded the textbook—and here he was in a cubicle!

Poet Philip Levine!

Philip Levine and My Pursuit of a Life in Poetry

JOSEPH O. LEGASPI

In the fall of 1996, the start of my final year of graduate studies in the Creative Writing Program at New York University, I sat anxiously at a long table in a shabby conference room for my poetry workshop with Philip Levine. I was about to come face-to-face and study with a poet whose reputation for being tough, hard-nosed, and candid preceded him. My trepidation, however, was tempered with giddy excitement because I had admired Philip's poems for years. They spoke to me like none other: "What Work Is," "You Can Have It," "Starlight," "They Feed They Lion" . . . His work influenced my own work and love of poetry. For me it was a monumental honor just to be in that workshop. The sentiment emanated from my peers as well, the room rife with nervous shuffling and muffled anticipation. Who arrived and presided over the class that first evening was the enigma we expected: a man with bite, direct in his ways, dismissive in his low tolerance for bullshit. *Curmudgeon* came to mind. But truly, it was a refreshing turn. At that crucial stage of my being a poet, I needed a good jostling, a firm shakedown. Quickly we learned that this man revered poetry and he would instill this reverence in us. And by semester's end we'd learn—surprisingly, since we were young and did not possess such telescopic foresight—that Philip cared immensely for his students. Not all of us survived: a handful of students dropped out during the early weeks of the semester. Transferred into less demanding, tough-love–averse workshops. But for those of us who stuck it out, we received a profound education in truth seeking and truth telling.

I wrote the least during my semester with Philip. But it was also when I learned the most, when I worked the hardest. My classmates and I developed sensitivity in every sense: thick skin and heartbeats. Since he demanded the best from each and every one of his students, Philip reprimanded us for passable work, for lazy writing. Initially, I wrote to please him—the way one tries to please a father, to avoid a scolding. But he saw through that. He then challenged me to believe in my voice, to write as a way of necessary nourishment, and to delve into subjects that are important to me. Philip pushed me to construct my poems beyond the self, to think about my work as it relates to history and the social condition, to view things in a larger, broader context. At the same time, there was a new intensity in my focus and attention to my writing. *Is this true?*, I'd ask, as I strove for not only factual accuracy, but emotional truth. Philip insisted on meticulous writing always. I began equating creating poems with hard work. This was a primary reason why it was my least prolific semester. Not that I'm a prolific writer to begin with, but I also learned to be more forgiving of myself. Furthermore, through his poems and teachings, Philip gave me license to write about the people in my life: working-class immigrants whose tiniest of lives were no less valid, complicated, and sacred. He dared me to get my hands dirty, digging down to such depths to unearth truth.

Because of his narrative aesthetic, subject matter, and rigor, it was then apparent that I needed to work with Philip on my thesis. Aesthetically and politically, we meshed. He was a paradigm of work ethic. With him I could see that I might have a place in poetry. Even though he was not teaching the spring semester and was under no obligation to NYU's Creative Writing Program, Philip took three to four graduating students under his wing. As our thesis advisor, he made himself readily available and met with each one of us frequently. I treasured my sessions with Philip. They were not completely about grueling poetics and thesis work, either. Many times we simply talked about our lives. Possessing wit and wisdom, Philip was a great storyteller with an anecdote for every turn in the conversation. Here was a man who led an interesting, adventurous life. We talked about politics and mused over art and literature. Apart from providing critiques on my poems, he doled out advice on how to live a life in poetry. Foremost, Philip advised me to take care of myself, bodily and spiritually. He shared lessons learned from his past. He told me not to buy into the outdated notion of poets as drunks and addicts and wayward, depressive loners. As someone brought up as a good Catholic boy, I was worried about not having enough gritty material. But my life and the earth contain plenty of fodder for creative work. Simple and obvious, perhaps, but it was something an upstart, a man in his early twenties, needed to hear. Our sessions served as an outlet for me to confront and understand my life more fully, to broaden my reach. Some of our talks cut to the core. There were times I left our one-on-one conferences in tears, emotionally spent, but enlightened. These episodes were primarily triggered by disclosures about my family, my past, and my childhood in a foreign land. In Philip's presence and with his counsel, I opened up about the difficulties and pain of immigrant lives—my guilt over the sacrifices my parents had made to provide for their now distant, Westernized children. I had an excellent, big-hearted listener in Philip, a wise survivor. I felt such an overwhelming sense of intimacy that I'd never felt with an elder. Then there was this creative writing business, sheer luxury for a Filipino-American boy from a working-class family in which survival was the modus operandi. I left Los Angeles to pursue what? Poems. For years, I told my family I studied (and eventually received a degree in) journalism, something they could digest and understand. In Philip I had someone who championed poetry. He encouraged me and made me believe that this was a noble undertaking.

After graduate school, I kept in touch with Philip predominantly through the postal service. Of course I saw him at readings and literary events, where he was always happy to see his former students, but those situations were not at all conducive to catching up. The mail became our mode of correspondence. His schedule and health permitting, Philip's turnaround responses were timely. His letters contained taciturn and whimsical anecdotes from his life. Often he included much-appreciated encouragements for my poetry. Upon leaving NYU, I had to make ends meet living in New York City. I fell into a public relations job that zapped my creative time and energy. I was struggling to balance my life. Philip's letters offered motivation. They seemed to tell me: *I believe in your work. You are doing fine.* At the time, I needed such blessings, especially from the poet whom I consider my father in poetry. Because of our correspondence, I remained connected to poetry.

I did not expect to develop a continued relationship with my professors at NYU beyond my matriculation. Indeed, I will cherish those two years for the rest of my life. But to be taught and cared for by Philip Levine is the most substantial gift. His mentoring transcends time and circumstance. When I needed a renowned poet to write a foreword for my debut collection, I wrote Philip a letter with my request, and within a week or so a letter arrived with the great news that he had agreed to do it. What a wonderful foreword he wrote, too! If I manage to publish only my one book, I'm fulfilled. But I have much to be grateful for. Philip has emboldened me to follow my passion despite my social and cultural obstacles—to be determined in my pursuit. Philip has ushered me into a life in poetry.

Philip Levine

A Resonant Presence

MARI L'ESPERANCE

Phil Levine was my teacher on the page long before we met in person. When I came to writing poetry, I was nearly thirty—late by some standards—and discovering Phil's poems for the first time (in adult continuing education classes, following dull days at office jobs in downtown San Francisco) was akin to opening a door onto a forgotten part of myself. Phil's poems of empathy, witness, and emotional truth connected me to the working-class world of my father's New England childhood during the Great Depression—a world where internal and external resources were scarce, anger flared quickly and too often, and a different kind of life seemed remote and unattainable. In those early years of familiarizing myself with poetry and stumbling toward my own poems, Phil's poems were not only models for what art could be made of, but for how a life in poetry could be fed, shaped, and made real. For a young poet writing her first poems in the dark, this was a tremendous revelation.

Sometime later, when I was a second-year graduate student at New York University, Phil came to teach in the fall of 1995. I was reeling from the unexplained disappearance of my mother the previous semester and felt numb and disoriented in my grief; for some months it had taken everything in me simply to function, let alone write poems. I can well recall the charged atmosphere as we anticipated Phil's arrival. It will not surprise anyone who is familiar with Phil as a teacher that his visit was preceded by his reputation (now its own mythology) as a tough critic who did not suffer fools and disdained wealth, privilege, and sloth. I once heard him say during a radio interview that in a poetry workshop there are a dozen people in a room and one of them is getting paid to tell the truth. For these reasons and more, some of my peers opted to study with other poets. I, on the other hand, was intrigued; this, after all, was the one and only Philip Levine! I signed on for the challenge. It turned out to be one of the best decisions of my life. My weekly classes with Phil provided me with a much-needed refuge of shared meaning and purpose at a time when I felt especially unmoored and vulnerable. I have no doubt the poems I wrote that semester, some of them keepers, were made possible by Phil's presence.

For those of us with apprehensions, Phil did not disappoint. On the first day of class, after the customary introductions and small talk, Phil asked who would like to share a poem. When no one jumped at the chance, I volunteered to be the first lamb sent to slaughter. I read my poem aloud to the group, then waited in the silence that fell over us, expecting the worst. After what felt like an eternity, although it was likely only a minute, Phil ventured, slowly and dryly, "Well . . . *this* poem has no future," glancing at me out of the corner of his eye as he uttered these words of doom. I sat quietly, swimming in my discomfort, yet determined not to flinch under Phil's gaze—determined to show him that I could take his heat, that I was big enough. I remained calm, my eyes fixed on the page in front of me as I waited for more. In time, Phil continued by telling us *why* my poem didn't have a future *as it was written* and gave me some suggestions for revision to consider, none of which I now remember. In fact, I remember very little else about that night. But by the end of it I was aware I had survived a kind of initiation, and felt secretly proud.

Phil was tough on us and on our poems because he believed we could do better, *be* better, and that if we applied ourselves and learned everything we could about poetry, as he had, our work would steadily improve. But I never experienced him as cruel, and he often tempered his feedback with sly humor and wisecracks, yet he always spoke his truth in service of the poem, bitter as that truth may have been to swallow. Phil's tough-love approach was not for everyone, and there were wounded feelings and disappointments. It's no secret that parental projections, not to mention sibling rivalries, abound in the crucible of any writing workshop. Depending on how each of us was feeling on a given day, Phil was a praising or critical father, a nurturing or rejecting mother, and every possible combination of these, and more. Whatever our individual experiences of him might have been, Phil was not there to make friends or cultivate an entourage; he was there to help us become the best poets we were capable of being at that nascent stage in our development.

I also delighted in Phil's stories, his now widely known accounts of studying at Stanford with a cantankerous Yvor Winters and at Iowa with the brilliant and eccentric John Berryman, and of his deep love and admiration for his student and colleague Larry Levis, whose posthumous collection *Elegy* Phil would edit the following year after Levis's untimely death at age forty-nine—a painful task. Often I think I benefited more from Phil's stories, from his warm and grounding presence, than I did from any feedback I received from him about my poems. I was becoming a poet through osmosis—we all were—and I eagerly inhaled and absorbed the poetry lore Phil shared with us. The lore connected me to something larger than myself: it connected me to the universal tradition and soul of poetry.

In preparation for this essay, I dug through old files to piece together what I could of that long-ago semester. I found old poem drafts with annotations in Phil's familiar spidery hand. In a spiral notebook I'd recorded dates and times of office-hour meetings that I can't now recall. Which brings me back to how dissociated I was at the time and how much Phil's workshop was an essential tether. That circle of poets with Phil at the helm, combined with my love of poetry, the knowledge that I had worked extremely hard to be able to study at NYU, and sheer will: these together somehow held me. I endeavored to make sense of my private loss (and it was mostly private, as I spoke to very few people about it) the only way I could: through poems that I brought to class each week. I have no doubt that Phil had some notion of what I was going through, although I never spoke to him about it and shared it with him only much later, in a letter. And, I'll admit now with some embarrassment, I was intimidated by the idea of contact with Phil outside of the classroom. What could I possibly say to him that would matter? I remember we all went out to a bar after class one night. Phil and Gerald Stern (who was also visiting that semester) had accompanied us, and both men sat off to the side while the rest of us drank and talked amongst ourselves. Even in that informal setting, I was too shy to approach Phil, to tell him how much his teaching and our class meant to me.

But in Phil's workshop, I was in my element. As a young poet I was steeped in doubt about my poems, and Phil let me know in his own way that he saw promise in what I was attempting to do, even though at the time I was not able to see it myself. He once said in class, half jokingly, in response to something I'd brought in: "This is great! Who wrote it?" I valued his humor, his forthrightness and integrity, and his willingness to speak to what was real, and these are qualities that still endear him to me and to those who love him. With Phil there was, and is, no bullshit, or tolerance of bullshit. Phil calls it as he sees it and that's an acquired taste for many. I ate it up. Maybe it helped that I was an older student who had been out in the world for a dozen years before entering graduate school, or that I, like Phil, was a product of a public university education who had traveled all the way from California to study poetry in New York City as a scholarship student. Whatever the case, I came to learn that, behind Phil's gruff persona, there was empathy and generosity, genuine love and caring, and an abiding devotion to the art and practice of poetry.

In subsequent years, when I was trying (often in vain) to write while making a living and grappling with the complicated, prolonged, and emotionally freighted circumstances related to my mother's disappearance (which remains unsolved), Phil repeatedly offered me encouragement and hope, reminding me to keep writing, to stay connected to my writer self, no matter what else might be going on in my life. Through a second round of graduate school and several years of professional training, I've been able to follow Phil's advice with uneven success, but this has not diminished his constancy and his significance to me as a teacher—a teacher not only in poetry, but also in life.

I did not meet Phil again for sixteen years, when he attended a reading I gave with a group of Fresno poets at Fresno State University in May 2011. When he approached me after the reading, I cried in disbelief and joy, followed by inarticulate attempts at speech. I'm not sure I could have read that night if I had known he was in the audience. Our encounter was brief, but meaningful. In his parting gift of a copy of *News of the World*, he'd written, "For Mari, with Hope," which says everything about what he has meant and continues to mean to me. A brief note he sent sometime later, which simply said, *I enjoyed your reading; you were quite wonderful*, buoyed me up for weeks.

I would venture to say we remember our most beloved teachers not as much for anything specific they've said about us or our work, but for their resonant presence in our lives and our psyches—an unnamable quality that, when we bring it into our awareness, reminds us, even across time and distance, that we and what we make have value and deserve to be in the world. It is this that I have treasured about Phil, and it has carried me through some painful estrangements from poetry and not having a sense that poems would ever return. Over the years Phil's letters of encouragement have sustained me. To this day, I reread them whenever I feel the need for his validating voice, his belief in me and my poems. Although our correspondence has been less frequent in recent years, Phil is never far from my thoughts and lives in my heart. I am deeply grateful to him and will never forget his kindness to me when I most needed it.

Winter, 1985

MARK LEVINE

It is unlikely I would have gone on to live my life in poetry, for better and worse, had I not taken a class with Philip Levine in 1985. I was nineteen at the time. I had never met a published writer, or an artist of any kind, and although I had read a small amount of poetry that had moved me deeply— *The Waste Land*, *Howl*, a few poems of Wallace Stevens, Sylvia Plath, Dylan Thomas—and had even, for some time, carried around a notebook of my own clumsy effusions, somehow it didn't occur to me that "poets" still existed, let alone that someone like me could aspire to be one.

I showed up at his class because his last name was the same as mine. It was the first day of the winter semester of my sophomore year, a Wednesday in January, three days after Ronald Reagan's second inaugural. I went to breakfast in the dark, empty dining hall and came across an article in a student newspaper about a visiting writer named Levine. I had gone to school with other kids named Levine, but their parents were dentists or accountants. My own Levines were a schoolteacher and a civil servant. According to the article, this Levine was a well-regarded poet. There was a picture of him: gap-toothed, with wavy, unkempt hair, a working man's mustache, and a nose that suggested a turbulent background. The class met at 1:00 in the chemistry building, which was on my way across campus. I had no hope of being allowed in—it was reserved, I imagined, for a small group of sophisticates—but I decided to stop by. A year earlier, I had shown up at a similar class to get a glimpse of Susan Sontag, and was quickly turned away.

The room was less crowded than I had expected. Levine wore tennis shoes and an old raincoat. I recall he joked about a student's ridiculous clear vinyl handbag inset with colorful plastic fish. The student seemed put off by the remark, and Levine happily referred to himself as a schmuck. He told us he was glad to have taken the job for the semester because he only had to show up on campus once a week and the salary was excellent. "I demanded what they had to pay me and they said, 'Levine, we can't pay you that much—you've only got a master's, everyone else has a doctorate and they make less.' And I told them, 'That's why I need to be paid more—you don't want to make me feel inferior because of my poor education.'"

He asked our names. I told him mine and he said: "That sounds familiar. I have a son who goes by that." Then he said, "Imagine how I must feel among friends with names like Justice and Galway Kinnell and W. S. Merwin"—he drew out the syllables, as though he were saying "Rockefeller" and "Vanderbilt" and "DuPont." "Lucky sons-of-bitches, put on earth with poets' names. And here I am, Phil Levine from Detroit." Someone asked about the procedure for applying to the class. He glanced around the room and said: "You look like nice people. You're in."

When I came back the next week, I was a few minutes late and had to climb over other students to an empty seat. Levine stopped talking and looked over at me. "Levine, you schmuck, get here on time," he said. He laughed. It was, I think, the first moment during my time in college that a teacher had addressed me with anything like personal regard. I began writing down everything he said. He wasn't like other professors. He spoke in little jabs, like a boxer, crisp and precise but without any concern for academic refinement. At the beginning of class he bit into an apple and he didn't stop eating until he had consumed the whole thing, core and all. He was blunt and categorical in his statements. He introduced the class to Hemingway's notion of a "shit detector." He pointed to the use of *azure* in a student's poem. "Question: when was the last time you heard the word 'azure'?" A few students fidgeted uncomfortably. "Answer:

the last time you did a crossword puzzle." There was something like a collective gasp in the room. We were accustomed to having teachers address us as "the best and the brightest." This was new. About half the students in class were veterans of the college literary scene and seemed to consider themselves members of a vanguard. Levine didn't coddle or equivocate. Fake language made bad poems. He mocked pretension. Another student read aloud her poem in a tone full of silences, exclamations, urgencies. The writer's circle of friends took turns celebrating her. After a pause, Levine spoke: "I heard better language coming over on the bus this morning."

He seemed uninterested in interpreting poems, which was at first mystifying to a student like me, who had been trained to believe that the most valuable response to a poem was finding something clever or unexpected to say about it. He thought that the right words in the right sequence held a power that was magical and instantaneous. He read poems to us—W. B. Yeats, Thomas Hardy, Wilfred Owen, Elizabeth Bishop—with a passion I had never before encountered. His voice was rough and magisterial. Words were alive in him. He read with a clenched jaw, his body almost shaking. He described Keats's letters and made clear his sense that the imagination was a sacred place breeding authenticity in words. He insisted that the poem be lived. One student turned in a poem that used the word *lion* a single time, to symbolize power. Levine almost blew up. "Goddamn it," he shouted, "if you're going to put a poor lion in your poem, I want that lion to *be* there." He seemed to hunger after the texture of reality, which took many forms, but which was instantly recognizable to him. Another student's poem began: "A window. A baseball. The possibilities." It was a sparse and, in certain ways, abstract poem. He loved it. He saw a world in it: the object in flight, clean and clear; the suspension of time; the opening of imaginative possibility, of promised lands, however shattered, within the disappointments of the actual one.

Right away, it felt to me that Levine entered my life by the logic of dreams, bringing me to poetry when it was what I most needed, without having any idea I needed it. I had just returned to school following a five-week winter break in Toronto, where I grew up. There was heavy snowfall and bitter cold. My parents were both out of work for health reasons. My father had a spinal injury; my mother had been diagnosed with ovarian cancer the previous spring. They lived in a tiny two-bedroom house they had bought with the hope of enlarging, but construction had stopped when they ran out of money. By then, it was evident that my mother's rounds of chemotherapy had been unsuccessful, though the possibility she might die was never discussed. She was forty-nine years old and I was closer to no one. She spent most of that winter break in bed beneath an old Afghan in a cramped room whose only window had been boarded over during construction. One night my father took me aside and told me he had noticed a widening crack in a wall. He was certain that the load of snow and ice on the roof was going to lead to the collapse of the house. He told me he didn't want to alarm my mother with the news. Nonetheless, he said, he could think of nothing else. He hadn't slept in weeks.

The first poem I turned in to Levine's class was called "Racing." It started with a memory of racing my mother down the hallway of our apartment building when I was six years old. She would slow down toward the end of the hallway to allow me to arrive at the finish with her. "My mother's days have numbers on them," the poem began. It was full of shrill writing. It had many of the traits I believed poems were required to include: elaborate metaphor, compulsive vividness, heavy-breathing strains of high music. But it also had, it's possible, a trace of the inarticulate desperation I was living with. For a year, I had spoken to no one about my mother's illness, though it dominated my mind throughout every day. I certainly couldn't speak of it to my father. But I had managed, for the first time, to turn to poetry in an effort to specify emotions that were otherwise too harrowing for me to bear or to confront. Some connection I felt with this other Levine—born, uncannily, just a week before my father—had allowed me to do it. I deeply cared what he would say in class. He took the poem seriously. He was kind. He didn't patronize me. He told me what he liked and didn't like. He deflected the criticism of others in the class. He said, "Mr. Levine has work to do, but he has written the first draft of a genuine poem."

He began one class by asking, "Why do you write poetry?" Several students dared to answer. "To make something beautiful"—"To interrogate the dominant ideology"—"To give voice to the powerless." The student with the vinyl fish bag offered, "To get the bug out of my ear." Levine said: "There's only one reason to write poetry. To change the world."

He believed it. He believed poetry was the most important thing a person could do, and that poems bore the impulse for collective transformation without which lies and injustice would prevail. He loathed Reagan. He spoke of the crimes that politicians and capitalists had done to language. The right words mattered, he said, because poems could restore meaning to language. Poems were forbidden from lying.

Did some students find him cruel? Perhaps. His commitment was ferocious. He read aloud a poem by one of the literary stars of the campus. In Levine's voice, the poem, full of wordplay, ironic jabs, and references to literary theory, sounded spectacular. "Our friend Mr. D. has a flair for language," Levine said. "He's written something very smart, very knowing. It's charismatic and very appealing. It takes pains to show you what a wit the poet is. And if he continues this way, there's a good chance Mr. D. will never write a poem."

Week by week, though, it became clear that Levine was enjoying our group enormously, and the class developed both intimacy and boisterousness. Word got around, and visitors would come to sit in. Most everyone in the room was writing better, more ambitiously, more honestly, and Levine celebrated our small triumphs. He often reminded us how much he preferred us to the graduate students he met immediately after our class. "There's very little talent in that class," he told us. "Last week a student brought in a poem and asked, 'How can I make it better, Phil? How can I make it better?' And I said, 'There's only one way to make it better. Throw it away.'"

He was fifty-seven, but he was not famous and his bearing was embattled. "I didn't find my voice until I was older," he told us. "It was good for me to have the time to work at becoming a poet, and it would be good for you, too. But by the time I was thirty-five and still didn't have a book, I'd had enough, and I was in danger of becoming a real asshole."

Less than halfway through the semester, I returned to Toronto. My mother was in the hospital. I spent the next three weeks in her room. She suffered tremendously. She put up with one monstrous procedure after another in an effort to live marginally longer. I had terrible fights with my father. A stream of visitors came to the room, draining my mother of what energy she had. I had a poem folded in my pocket that I wanted to read to her, but I couldn't find the right moment. Just before she died, as a nurse was struggling to prod a needle into a vein, my mother turned to me and said, "To hell with it."

I returned to school. In the dining hall, before Levine's class, I wrote a draft called "Poem for My Birthday, April 17, 1985." "I have shoveled gravel onto our muddy driveway / To keep the mourners' cars from sinking, / Spreading the stones with my old hockey stick," I wrote. I brought the poem to class. Levine's presence, his voice, his vision of poetry, had become something of a lifeline for me. After class I went to the bookstore and bought his *Selected Poems* as a birthday present for myself. It was the first book I owned by a living poet. I had never seen such poems: "Baby Villon," "Silent in America," "Animals Are Passing from Our Lives," "Zaydee," "1933." I was overwhelmed. The work was living proof of what I had been hearing in his class: that art could be made out of forceful, hard-won, everyday language; that poems didn't have to decide between rage and humor, sorrow and joy; that the imagination gave access to a larger life. I hadn't imagined that one could write poetry as an unapologetic urban Jew—not a toney, long-assimilated German Jew, but one of the more recently arrived, a child of Yiddish-speaking, tenement-dwelling Russian and Polish Jews, shopkeepers and laborers, who didn't have fine manners, who were overconcerned with money, who argued loudly and ate bad food and sometimes got sick and died young and were inconsolable. A Levine.

A few weeks later, I showed up to the last class. It was a beautiful spring day. Levine was all smiles. "I'm feeling great," he told the group. "I just picked up my paycheck." I brought in a new poem called "My Milieu," about being on vacation with my parents when I was fifteen. "In other times," it began, "My parents and I woke early / To eat at a bar, / A ninety-five-cent meal / On stools." It was, I think, a hard thing for me to have written, let alone to have brought to class: a poem about being embarrassed by my parents; about being attached to them; about belonging to a family that was gone. The poem ended, "They liked the food, / For them it was / Eating out." My draft of the poem has my handwritten transcription of the class discussion. One student said, reasonably enough: "I don't believe it. It feels pretentious." Another observed, "It's about the relationship of the self to particular societal classes." Levine responded, "What it's about is how difficult it is to live, to live as a young person and then to live as an old person." He recommended I read Rimbaud's "Poet at Seven." He added, "I may be wrong—this poem may be a piece of shit." Several members of the class challenged the poem for its cynicism. Levine interrupted. "You know, people often call my poems cynical," he said. "They say, 'Levine, why are you so damn cynical? Why must you be so cynical?' And I say, 'Fuck you. I'm not being cynical, I'm being realistic.'"

After class, I got my courage up to ask him whether we could have a beer together. It wasn't possible that day, he said, but we would find a time to do it soon. He told me I could send him a few poems in the mail when I felt ready to do it. He had given me his honest attention when I needed it, and he would step back and let me be free of his influence when that was what was called for. It's what one would hope for, but rarely would receive, from a teacher or from a parent. A month later I was back in Toronto. It was a difficult time. That June, I received Levine's written evaluation of my class work. It was a more than generous paragraph. Its last words shocked me and changed the course of my life. "He could make his mark as a poet," Levine wrote.

Philip Levine

LARRY LEVIS

1

To attempt to be at all objective about my friend and my first teacher Philip Levine is impossible for me. For to have been a student in Levine's classes from the mid to late 1960s was to have a life, or what has turned out to be my life, *given* to me by another. And certainly then, at the age of seventeen, I *had* no life, or no passionate life animated by a purpose, and I was unaware that one might be possible.

Let me explain: by the age of sixteen I was already a kind of teenage failure, an unathletic, acne-riddled virgin who owned the slowest car in town, a 1959 Plymouth sedan that had fins like irrelevant twin sharks rising above the taillights. Beige, slow as driftwood, the car became interesting only when I cut the engine and lights to coast down a hill in full moonlight outside town as I drove home to the ranch, listening to the wind go over the dead metal and sitting there in the self-pity of adolescence, a self-pity so profound that it made me feel, for a moment anyway, at once posthumous and deliciously alive.

Had I been good at something, had my times in the 400-yard freestyle and 100-yard breaststroke actually not grown worse over four years, had I had a girlfriend or a chopped and channeled Merc with a V-8, I would not have read poetry. But I did read it, because a teacher named Maranda showed me Frost's poems, and I couldn't shake them or rid my mind of them.

One night I wrote a poem. I think I actually composed it while listening to music, to some sticky orchestrated sound track from a movie. The poem was awful of course; even I knew that. It was awful except for one thing. It had one good line in it. I was sixteen then, almost seventeen, almost a senior, and about important things I did not deceive myself. One good line at the age of sixteen was a lot. I decided then that I would go to sleep, and if the line was still good in the morning, then I would become a poet. I remember thinking that I might qualify the decision by saying that I would try to become a poet. The word *try* seemed dead of exhaustion. No, that was no good, I thought immediately. One either did this or did not do it.

When I got up, I looked at the line. It was still good.

Everything crucial in my life had been decided in less than thirty seconds, and in complete silence.

My great good fortune came a few months later disguised as a grade of D in my photography class. That dark mark meant I could not go to Berkeley or to any University of California campus. I tried to persuade my teacher, Mr. Ferguson, that most students thought the course was a kind of joke. This turned out to be the wrong argument. And in fact I deserved the grade, for I had hardly attended the class. I hated the smells of developing fluids and fixers and would hang back with my friend Zamora while the other students filed into the darkroom, then slip out the door and sit smoking cigarettes with him in the empty stadium bleachers. We spoke exclusively of girls, of what wonders must be concealed beneath Colleen Mulligan's cashmeres or within Kathy Powell's white dress. I sat there smoking and earning my D. The D meant I would have to go to Fresno to attend college. Yes, Fresno. Dust and Wind State.

How lucky I was, though my little destiny was completely disguised as failure, for at Fresno State I would spend the next four years in Levine's poetry workshops, although I could not have known that then, smoking with Zamora. No one knew anything then. It was 1964. A few years later Zamora would for some reason wander away from the others on his patrol somewhere in Vietnam and come home in a body bag.

I don't know what happened to Colleen Mulligan, but I saw Kathy Powell years later at a reunion. She had moved to Ketchum, Idaho, and was still beautiful. She had been reading a book of poems by Sharon Olds and asked me about them. At seventeen I would never have imagined that she would ever want to read poetry, for I thought the untroubled life of the beautiful lay before her and that it needed no poems.

At seventeen, I knew so little.

I do know that it was Philip Levine who saved my life. I don't know if anyone could have saved Zamora's. Two years ago, I finally touched the name cut into the black stone of the Vietnam War Memorial along with the other fifty thousand. Zamora was a Chicano who worked long hours after school at a variety of demeaning jobs, and had, perhaps, outgrown all self-pity by the age of seven.

We sat there smoking, me with my invisible great good luck, and Zamora, as it turned out, without any. "All I want for Christmas is to get in her pants," he sang, idly, and flipped his cigarette butt past twenty rows of empty seats.

2

It isn't enough to say that Levine was a brilliant young poet and teacher. Levine was amazing. His classes during those four years at Fresno State College were wonders, and they still suggest how much good someone might do in the world, even a world limited by the penitentiary-like architecture and stultifying sameness of a state college. For in any of those fifty-minute periods, there was more passion, sense, hilarity, and feeling filling that classroom than one could have found anywhere in 1964. If the class was difficult, if Levine refused to coddle students or protect the vanities of the lazy and mediocre from the truth about their work, if his criticism was harsh at times, all of this was justified and beautiful: justified because some students thought that an A could be had for repeating the clichés on greeting cards or that everything they did would be judged as mildly as finger painting in grade school; and it was beautiful because there poetry was given the respect it deserves and was never compromised to appease the culture surrounding it in the vast sleep of its suburbs, highways, and miles of dark packing sheds (all of which, I might add, if left without the intelligence and beauty of art, is in its mute entirety absolutely worthless).

But beneath the difficulty of the class, of studying and writing in traditional prosody, beneath the harshness of the criticism Levine gave to us, impartially and democratically, there was in the way he taught a humor and a talent for making the most self-conscious young students laugh at themselves and at their mistakes; by doing so, they could suddenly go beyond the uselessly narrow, brittle egos they had carried with them since junior high like a life savings in the wrong currency; that laughter woke them from the sleep of adolescence into something far larger. What was larger was the world of poetry, not only the study of it (passionate rather than impartial in Levine's readings of it), but also the possibility of writing it. If you could forget awhile your whining, hungry, sulking selves, Levine seemed to say to us, you could enter this larger world where the only president was Imagination. Levine made this the necessary world. And doing this made him unforgettable. It was a class like no other if only because it dared all of us in it to be considerably more alive than we wanted to be. In this sense it couldn't be compared to anything else I took there. In French 2B, for example, we recited a paragraph from *Eugenie Grandet* in French, and then once again, translated, in English. Nothing had changed in the format of French 2B since Charlemagne. My French professor was named Wesley Byrd. The one time I stopped in to see him during his office hours he was totally absorbed in plucking his eyebrows before a small hand mirror propped on his desk, and he did not pause in doing this even momentarily as he asked me to come in. "Professor Byrd," I asked, after a short interchange concerning the due date of a term paper, "after Rimbaud, did the alexandrine line disappear from French verse?" "Yes," he replied, snipping away, "gradually, it did." Then I asked, "What do you think of Rimbaud?" "Rimbaud?" he replied, going after another longish and troublesome stray hair; "Rimbaud was a flash in the pan." His pronouncement, his "sentencing," was unhesitating and final, and I never asked him anything else. The difference between Levine and Byrd, both at the same college, is like the difference between the music of John Coltrane and Doc Severinsen. One is amazing and a revelation; the other makes you wonder who hired him.

Levine was the funniest and most unflinchingly honest man I have ever known. In those years, class after class would literally shake with laughter. A kind of rare, almost giddy intelligence constantly surfaced in Levine in comments that were so right and so outrageous that they kept us all howling, for he kept brimming over with the kind of insouciant truths most people suppress in themselves, and none of us in the class were spared from those truths about our work, and, by extension, about ourselves. "Amazing! You write like the Duke of Windsor on acid!" he said to one passively stoned, yet remarkably pompous student. Or, to another: "For a moment there your imagination made an appearance in this poem and its loveliness astonished us all, but then . . . right . . . *here*—where you say, 'Love is golden, Daddy, and forever,' the grim voice of Puritan duty comes back in and overwhelms you with a sense of obligation even you couldn't possibly believe in. Remember, in poetry you don't owe anyone a thing." Or: "Look at this absolutely gorgeous line crying out to escape from all its dumb brothers snoring beside it there!" Or, to a young woman who had written a wonderfully sophisticated poem about a detested ski instructor: "'With practiced stance which he has made his own'—notice all of you please, in the deafness of this age, this line. It's amazingly perfect for what it's doing here, lean, scrupulous, and innocent in tone at the outset. And, just now, it's a pentameter that seems to be light-years beyond anything the rest of you can do. Oh, I know you *have* ears, I mean, I can see them right there on the sides of your heads, and yet on some days they strike me as vestigial, like the appendix, and as the age evolves I can see them creeping toward extinction; soon, all that will be left of ears will be their occasional appearance on postage stamps, along with the passenger pigeon, the Great Auk, Adlai Stevenson." Or, to a student full of pretentiously profound yet completely trite statements concerning God, Love, Death, and Time—a two-page endeavor with all the lines italicized in the typescript: "Writing like this suggests that you might need to find something to do with your hands. Tennis is an excellent sport!"

Something animated him. He is the only person I have ever known who seemed to be fully awake to this life, his own and the lives of others. An amazing talker, it surprised me when I noticed how deeply and closely he listened to students. And when someone was really troubled, a special kind of listening seemed to go on, and there was often a generous if sometimes unsettling frankness in his response.

Why in the world did he care so much about what we did? Because we mattered so much to him, we began to matter to ourselves. And to matter in this way, to feel that what one did and how one wrote actually might make a difference, was a crucial gift Levine gave to each of us. All you had to do was open it, and it became quite clear, after awhile, that only cowardice or self-deceit could keep you from doing that.

His care for us seems all the more amazing when I recall that these years were crucially difficult and ultimately triumphant years for him as a poet. For in 1965 he went to Spain for the first time, and what changed him deeply there is apparent everywhere in the poems of *Not This Pig*. Shortly after this, he would begin to write the poems that constitute the vision of *They Feed They Lion*. What still strikes me as amazing, and right, and sane, was his capacity to share all that energy, that fire, with those around him: students and poets and friends. The only discernible principle I gathered from this kind of generosity seems to be this: to try to conserve one's energy for some later use, to try to teach as if one isn't quite there and has more important things to do, is a way to lose that energy completely, a way, quite simply, of betraying oneself. Levine was always totally there, in the poems and right there in front of me before the green sea of the blackboard.

3

It is fashionable now to disparage poetry workshops, and why not? Some of them are so bad that they constitute a form of fraud in which mediocre talents accept tuition from those with no talent whatsoever. After a couple of years, these unemployables graduate, and their teachers, in their aspiring emptiness, get promoted. But to categorically condemn all workshops as a destructive force in our poetry is nonsense, a nonsense best said on a cliff overlooking the ocean at, say, Big Sur, where one can pretend, momentarily, to be Jeffers or some other great American Original. And much of Jeffers is just awful. How could a man who looked like that in the photos of him on display at Nepenthe write such dull stuff? Was there no one to tell him how bad it was? In contrast, I think of Pound showing Ford Madox Ford some early work, and of Ford laughing so hard upon reading it (they were not humorous poems) that he actually fell onto the floor and rolled around on it squealing with hilarity at the poems. Pound said that Ford's laughter saved him two years of work in the wrong direction. That was a poetry workshop. That laughter, no matter how painful for Pound, was a useful laughter, even a necessary laughter.

Could I have written poems in isolation? I doubt it. I grew up in a town where, in the high school library, Yeats's *Collected Poems* was removed, censored in fact, because two students had been found laughing out loud at "Leda and the Swan." That left Eliot. For two years, largely in secret, I read and reread Eliot, and I told no one of this. But finally one afternoon in journalism class, while the teacher was out of the room, Zamora stretched out, lying over three desktops, and began yelling at the little, evenly spaced holes in the plyboard ceiling: "O Stars, O Stars!" The others around us talked on in a mild roar. Then Zamora turned to me and said: "I saw that book you always got with you. Once again, guy, I see through you like a just wiped windshield." There was this little pause, and then he said, "What is it, you wanna be a poet?" I said, "Yeah. You think that's really stupid?" His smile had disappeared by the time he answered: "No, it isn't stupid. It isn't stupid at all, but I'd get out of town if I were you."

It was true. A town like that could fill a young man with such rage and boredom that the bars of Saigon might twinkle like a brief paradise. You could die in a town like that without lifting a finger.

Whenever I try to imagine the life I might have had if I hadn't met Levine, if he had never been my teacher, if we had not become friends and exchanged poems and hundreds of letters over the past twenty-five years, I can't imagine it. That is, nothing at all appears when I try to do this. No other life of any kind appears. I cannot see myself walking down one of those streets as a lawyer, or the boss of a packing shed, or even as the farmer my father wished I would become. When I try to do this, no one's there; it seems instead that I simply had never been at all. All there is on that street, the leaves on the shade trees that line it curled and black and closeted against noon heat, is a space where I am not.

Worth Fighting For

An Essay for Philip Levine

ADA LIMÓN

The reason I wanted to go to New York University to get my Master of Fine Arts in Poetry was so that I might get the chance to study with Sharon Olds and Philip Levine. Sharon Olds's poems came to me in high school and nearly gutted me without warning. Levine's poems came to me two years later when I worked at my local bookstore, Readers' Books in Sonoma, during the summer of 1995. A nationwide contest centered around the PBS series "The Power of the Word" would bring the television journalist Bill Moyers to the winning town's poetry festival. Beating out places like New York City, Sonoma's Poetry Festival won. Bill Moyers came to our small town and even shook my hand. I was nineteen. Everything was amazing. Along with Moyers came a slew of wonderful poets including Levine. When Levine read I was wonderstruck. He was a smaller man than I expected, but he was serious and powerful, and his voice was a pounding power tool and was beautifully muscled. I was completely enthralled by his poems and the sheer force of him.

Later, during my junior year of college, I took a poetry class and rediscovered Levine, first with "They Feed They Lion" (I walked around saying "Earth is eating trees" over and over for a month), and then with all his books, which I inhaled one by one. In my second poetry class, we watched a video of an interview with Levine. He terrified me. And also, I liked him very much. Somehow, he reminded me of the men I knew growing up: hard, quick-witted, smart, and honest.

Needless to say, my very first graduate class at NYU, in the old building that was all yellow with dim lights and dim walls and dim rooms, was led by the great Philip Levine himself. I remember seeing his name on my class schedule and not quite believing it. I was so nervous that I showed up an hour early. I tried not to act as nervous as I was. I sat on my hands and I leaned forward. I was twenty-three years old. I hadn't been an English major in college. Most of what I knew about poetry was from the Bill Moyers series, the few beginning courses at the University of Washington, the books I read while I worked at the bookstore during summers, and instinct. I felt highly unprepared.

Levine began the class by asking whether anyone smoked. No one raised a hand, either out of fear or out of shock at the question. He then said, "Well, if no one smokes, we won't need to take breaks!" Then, he started the class. I was sitting in the seat directly to his left and I couldn't help staring at him. He began with general advice. He even talked about learning to live in New York, which was helpful for me since I had come from the West Coast and this class was occurring approximately three days after my arrival. But mostly, I couldn't hear what he was saying. I was sitting a foot a way from Philip Levine and I was so overwhelmed by his presence and the pressure I felt to remember the moment as clearly as possible, I don't think I heard a word.

When it came to workshopping poems, he was surprisingly generous with mine in the beginning. I wrote pretty straightforward narrative poems that had a beginning, a middle, and an end. I had no idea what I was doing, but I tried to mimic famous poets as much as I could. I would read a poem, and then I would write a poem in a similar vein. They weren't great poems, but they were starter-poems, poems that were teaching me how to write a poem. Levine seemed to understand that and thought, perhaps, I was on the right track. Nothing in my life up until that moment could compare with the feeling of sitting next to Philip Levine while he held one of my new poems in his not-new hands. He read. I studied the tiny movements of his face, looking for any sign of approval. It was agonizing. It was exhilarating. Sometimes, however, it was devastating. I'm not being dramatic, though it sounds like

I am. I was just barely an adult; if someone didn't like a poem, and if that person happened to be Philip Levine, oh yes, it was devastating.

After spending an afternoon in Central Park, having walked there from Union Square (forty-five blocks with a backpack full of books, still nervous about getting lost on the subway), I fell in love with some Kenneth Koch poems. And so, that week I attempted to write a poem that was similar to his lovely poem "The Magic of Numbers." I had random train numbers and letters and times and little fragments in between them. I can't remember what I called it, but it was two pages and it was scattered and rambling and I thought it was terribly innovative and expansive; Levine, however, did not.

When I brought the poem in, I was probably the proudest I had ever been of a poem. And when Levine read it, he simply said, "This is not a poem." I don't remember much of what he said after that; the blood pounding in my brain was drowning out any further criticism. In an effort to defend me, and if you know him, to defend all literature that veers outside the traditional narrative, Kazim Ali said, "But don't you think there are some beautiful lines here?" To which Levine responded, "Oh sure, there are some beautiful lines, I just wish she'd put them in a fucking poem."

That night, I drank too much with friends outside a bar near Union Square and I started to tell them why he was wrong, and how the long lines I was using was something I was trying, and though it was new for me, I felt like it was going to be important. The next morning, sour with alcohol, I remembered one of the things Levine had told us the very first day, that he would give his opinion, his honest opinion of a poem, he wouldn't sugarcoat it, and from that we would learn what to improve upon, but most importantly, we would also learn what to fight for. I knew then I was going to fight for my long, rambling conversational lines, and I did. The long lines are the big talk, the reaching out and going on and on, and I wanted to keep them. I wouldn't have known that, if it weren't for Levine. He made me pick the one thing that I could salvage from that poor, anemic, Koch-inspired poem, and spend my life working on it.

What was undeniably evident about Levine's teaching style, and the way he ran a workshop, was that in order to learn how to be a better poet, you needed to learn how to be a tougher poet. He wouldn't tolerate the thin skin or inflated egos—especially in those of us in our early twenties—that were so prevalent in creative writing programs. He knew that at our very best, we were young, sensitive tuning forks vibrating in the world for the first time, and at our worst, we were egomaniacal wimps that couldn't stomach the real world so we hid behind sad windows and sadder words. What he wanted from us was something real and tangible. He wanted us to go outside of ourselves and say something that was true in a way that no one could deny. He wanted risk, not risk in terms of form, but risk in terms of honesty. When he'd come across a poem that struck a nerve, you could see his eyes brighten and glow with excitement. It was a look we all longed for constantly. It was a look worth writing (and failing) for.

I began to bring poems to Levine's office hours. Once the fellow poet Shane Book told me that Levine always kept his office hours and hardly anyone took advantage of it. So, I began to go every chance I could. He always had a yogurt and a banana in a paper bag and seemed (how unlikely!) extraordinarily accessible. I went in with a poem about my stepfather once, called "Simple Pleasures." (The word *simple* was no doubt lifted from Levine's book *The Simple Truth*.) I came in and tried to be casual, saying, "I think this poem may be too sentimental, will you take a look?" He replied, "I don't even have to look at it, it probably is." Still, he read the poem and told me places where it worked and places where it didn't. He liked that the whole premise of the poem was about a man taking two half-full egg cartons and combining them into one, a perfect dozen. Then, we talked about New York and how broke I was, and scared, and how I had no idea what I was going to do afterward and Levine listened. When I left, I felt like I was going to be a better poet, and maybe even survive my first year in New York City. He told me to move to Brooklyn and I did.

Toward the end of my semester with Levine, I was doing something I hadn't done before, I was really truly *working* on poems. I wasn't letting them simply come out in some wild burst of unnamable energy; instead, I wrote drafts and drafts and began to craft and edit and focus on the real artistry of the work rather than on the sometimes too-raw fever of the work. What was happening was that I was starting to take writing poetry seriously. I was starting to fight for my own voice. I was becoming both brave and vigilant. I no longer relied on the fire alone; I was learning to control where it burned, how it burned, and how long the glow would last. It was something entirely new and I was becoming addicted to it. To this day, I'm not sure whether any of that would have happened if Levine hadn't been my first, and very fiery, teacher.

Since then, Levine and I have shared a few postcards. I've sent him each book as it has come out, with thanks to him always. I don't think my books would exist if it weren't for him, for his sometimes harsh and growling criticism, for his gentle, kind laugh and witty banter, for telling it like it is, at least like it is for him. He never promised that he would teach us to be poets, but at least for me, he certainly taught me how to really want to be a poet with all my being.

Levine also told all of us to go out to a bar and get some drinks together. It seemed an offhand comment at the time, but it wasn't. Up until then, most of us would walk home alone after class, stare out train windows, think how hard words were, but when Levine said, "It's part of your job to go out and drink and talk to each other," that's what we did. We drank and talked and wrote better poems for it and made better friends for it. My classmates gave me books to read, and suddenly a whole different world of poetry was opening. For Levine, poetry was what you did in silence, but the conversation about poetry was a lively living thing, an energetic "Let's have one more" thing, and it was those nights out at the Stoned Crow that truly bonded me to the life of poetry and to the poetry community.

I still think a great deal of what he told me about putting the lines into a "fucking" poem. It reminds me to constantly put the poem first, that the endgame is the complete piece that you deliver to an audience. No matter how important the details are, the bigger movement of the poem, the essential arc and heart of the poem always have to come first. He taught me to value the work that it takes, to acknowledge and bow down to the art that we work in service of every day. In his class, I learned that poetry doesn't come easily, that the life of a poet is not easy, but what you give up to attain it will always pale in comparison to the true joy of living a life dedicated to art. And for that lesson alone, there are no words to express just how tremendously grateful I am. Levine offered a way to learn how to balance an overwhelming tenderness toward the world (that I believe most artists feel in some ways) with an exacting, tough, and unforgiving truth. I'm not embarrassed to admit how often I return to his first teachings even now, nearly twelve years after I entered a classroom and sat down to study words with a true incomparable master, for that is where I began my real life in service to the art of poetry.

Phil Levine at Houston

My First Teacher

ELLINE LIPKIN

In the late 1990s I knew I'd had enough of New York. Done with stuffing myself inside my tiny studio apartment, set like a Lite-Brite peg inside an anonymous building grid; done with my MFA, but not yet done with school, I was clearly ready for a change.

All of these factors landed me in Houston, Texas, in the fall of 1997, ready to start the doctoral program in creative writing and literature. The air was so swampy with thick humidity it seemed to vibrate in waves around my body as if I had walked into a Keith Haring drawing. I moved into a spacious one-bedroom apartment that rented for less than half of the cost of my West Village mousehole and kept waiting for someone from the management office to knock at the door and explain that a zero had been left off the monthly rental price. Shockingly, no one ever did. I unpacked my books while keeping close to the air conditioner lodged in the living room window like a framed ice cube that I prayed would never melt. Eagerly, apprehensively, I got ready for my first day of school.

Prospective students had been told that Richard Howard would be leaving Houston's faculty and his replacement hadn't yet been determined. The day before I was due to fly out from New York, I ran around my West Village neighborhood in a flurry of last-minute Goodwill donations, box mailing, and general panic when I spotted Richard Howard walking toward me on the street. He was unmistakable, with his characteristic glasses and portly girth. I briefly considered, but then quickly dismissed, saying something to him. Yet the literal crossing of our paths seemed symbolic.

Mid-summer, I had learned that Philip Levine would be Howard's fall replacement, hence my first workshop teacher in Houston. I had been a fan of Phil's work for years and had heard him read down by Manhattan's waterfront at Battery Park the summer before, not long after finishing my MFA at Columbia. The title poem to his collection *What Work Is* had already become a favorite. The longing in the poem, the alchemy of despair and of love, of rage against the industrial machine coupled with profound connection to what seemed to be both a literal and a universal brother, had affected me deeply. And the mere phrase *what work is* stayed in my mind, turned over and over as I struggled with the value of making poems, as I both resented and resisted my dull, grey-cubicle job, as I raged to find a place for myself within the crush of the city.

During his reading I was surprised at how funny Phil could be in his between-poem patter, but then how his tone shifted and his whole demeanor changed as he began to read, sliding into a voice that was both serious and hard, full of iron and grit, like his subjects, yet still warm and lambent. There was a conviction at the root of each poem, a mineral truth that had to come out, and I felt it in my bones. I didn't know how to characterize it, but it seemed like a timbre of humanity resided in his voice as he read—something metallic and essential emerged in his tone. It struck me, as I sat on an uncomfortable lawn chair, like the sound our voices tried to make at the end of a yoga class when the instructor encouraged us, jaded Manhattanites, to *om* together in harmony. I knew Phil would think that was ridiculous, as I did too, at least a little bit. But the vibration in his voice truly seemed to resonate at another frequency, one that held the spirit of poetry and then let it fly out through his words.

When I learned that Phil would be my teacher, I was both intimidated and thrilled. When that fateful first day of class came, our group assembled in a somewhat dingy classroom and waited for him to show up. A giddy nervousness ran throughout the room, and all chatter ceased as soon as he walked in, sat down, and began taking roll. What got under way that day was a workshop that started my career as a graduate student in Houston, but more so launched the seriousness I knew I wanted for poems, the core of which seeded my first book. We felt his belief in us as students, as poets, from the start, but it was clear that we would feel the boom of his critique clanging down on our heads as well. It was evident that he would not tolerate laziness of any kind.

But there was no need to worry. As a group we were so collectively eager to impress him and meet with his approval, the energy on that first day carried us through the whole semester. No one was late, and only dire sickness kept anyone from class. A healthy sense of competitive spirit prevailed. "I love coming here!" I remember a student bursting out one day; "this is a great workshop!" He was the person whom I had thought the most worldly, the most sophisticated, and the least impressionable.

During our workshop Phil sat at the head of the table, a beautiful fountain pen in hand, and, after the review, turned our drafts back to us with his precise script noting places to cut and to improve. He loved to tell stories, and quickly we all saw his gift for imitation. He would reminisce about a poet or about a time when he was a student of a particular teacher. Suddenly, he would turn his head and back around as far as he could swivel away from the class in his chair. When he then returned to face us, he was in character, acting out the encounter he wanted to share in the voice of whomever he was imitating. It was hysterically funny and entertaining, as his fond impersonations brought to life the anecdotes of his own education.

What I remember most from the camaraderie that developed over the semester's Tuesdays was Phil's profound humanity laid out on the table each week, offered up alongside a brutal honesty, warmth, and grit. He wanted what was best for us and if that meant telling someone that a line was disingenuous or full of horseshit, he certainly would do it. If something wasn't clear in a poem, he was going to say so. He referenced his pantheon of poet-stars who had spoken to him: Keats, Winters, Levis, and more, and he shared what had awed him, what he had learned starting out, never sugarcoating the difficult times, the hard years, the struggles that he faced, and how he found his way to the poems, all in hopes of getting us to go deeper into our craft.

Phil wanted us to pour ourselves into the work and to understand the elevation it could bring to us, but this would come through the intensity of our commitment. The path would surely be difficult, and he wasn't there to goad any illusions along, but rather to tell it to us straight; it would be a lonely, hard road that would not likely result in fame or fortune, to say the least. He roused us, he cajoled us, he encouraged us, and as needed, he disciplined us, too. But there was also the promise of a sense of fulfillment, of the joy of making art, and of the satisfaction of working hard at a craft.

Although he took us seriously as individuals, it was impossible for him to keep our names straight. He routinely mixed up our first names and would address one person by the name of a person across the room. He also had a baffling habit of calling all the women in the room "dear," a term I didn't mind, given his generation and his sincerity. As we approached the end of the semester, we collectively began to mourn the workshop's end. The only time in graduate school I ever experienced a spontaneous burst of applause from students at the end of a final class was after Phil paused, in the last five minutes of our last meeting, and with emotion in his voice told us how much he had enjoyed teaching us. We clapped to honor him, and with a gesture I had never yet seen from a teacher, he clapped back at us, saying he had to salute us as well.

At a celebratory dinner that night we lifted our glasses to him and thanked him for what we had each received—not only a deepening love for the work of poetry, but his belief in our work. After he gave his public reading that semester, I asked him to sign his books for me. Opening them to the front page, I was moved to see his inscription: "For one of my stars, one of my poets. With hope for the book to come." It is the underline that was most significant to me then, and still is now. We were his that semester as much as he was ours, and while we revered him, so he respected us, and even more meaningfully, he hoped for us. And that meant the world as we were all starting out.

At the reading I had bought one of the few books of Phil's that I didn't yet have, *The Simple Truth*. Onstage, he had joked about how his *Selected Poems* was a bargain and hawked his other books with good humor. He spoke kindly of Houston and the good time he'd had living in the city's swampy environment for the semester. And when I heard him read the title poem "The Simple Truth," there it was again—that grit and honesty, that tenderness and fierceness, all gathered somewhere in the hollow of his voice and harmonizing into something that rang in my body like an essential sound. "Can you taste what I'm saying?" he asks in the poem:

It is onions or potatoes, a pinch
of simple salt, the wealth of melting butter, it is obvious,
it stays in the back of your throat like a truth
you never uttered because the time was always wrong,
it stays there for the rest of your life, unspoken,

made of that dirt we call earth, the metal we call salt,
in a form we have no words for, and you live on it.

To me, it seemed like a touchstone from Phil—the phrase *the simple truth*—
meted out against all the complications likely ahead as I left the humid bubble
of my graduate school program. There might be despair and joblessness,
disappointment and rancor, but there was also a place to put these things—
to mark the tenderness, the vibrant moment, and to measure the distance
between these two. It was in the hollow, that timbre that opened up in his
poems and in his voice, and he was sharing this with us. He wanted this for
us, too. His critiques, his example, his encouragement all served me as I put
together my first collection, as I graduated, and as I made my way back out
into the workforce and into the largeness of the non-poetry-caring world,
trying to carry on the message I had received.

Years later, in Los Angeles, where I had settled more than ten years since
that first workshop, I heard Phil, recently named United States Poet Laure-
ate, read and then be interviewed onstage at the downtown public library.
His personality, his intensity, his warmth, and his essential irascibility came
flooding back. He riffed about the time he had stolen a book from a library,
and how much libraries had meant to him through the years. He recalled
being welcomed as a child by a librarian at his local branch. He was irrever-
ent as ever, humbled by and glad about his new position and the chance to
touch so many lives through poetry. He spoke of the amazing visit he'd had
to an elementary school classroom in upper Manhattan and the thrill he still
felt that sending poems out in the world could have such an effect. Funny,
critical, and irreverent, his ever unself-conscious edge came out, despite the
eminent visitors in the audience, as he good-humoredly began to let a hand-
ful of four-letter words fly.

When I shyly reintroduced myself to him at the signing, he thought for
a second and then said he remembered our class. He signed my book and
reached out to shake my hand. "Yes," he said, "that class had some fine poets
in it, and a seriousness that brought everyone up to a new level of writing."
I told him he had brought us to a new level of elevation, and I believed it.

Earlier, onstage in between poems, Phil had mentioned a student whose
work he had admired, who had been very talented, but who had died too soon.
The grief was present in his voice as he recollected him and read the poem
dedicated to him. "Students are never supposed to die before you do," Phil

said, "because you love them. You love them like children." This was another line that made me catch my breath. There it was again—the honesty, the willingness to bare his soul, and to face what's sharp-edged and hard; it dizzied me. And through his words I heard that tone—a steadiness of intensity, seasoned with salt, tempered by love. He had been my teacher for only one semester, but what I learned from him flooded back. "We'll be together in poetry," he inscribed in one of my books. There would always be this room, his message seemed to say, and he would always welcome us all in.

The Capricorn's Pedagogy

DANTE MICHEAUX

Great names were whispered throughout the newly renovated townhouse on West Tenth Street. Occasionally, a name became flesh as it dashed out the door and into a taxi or on foot to the grand literary life it led—or so I assumed. The house was a jewel and I was one of a small group of people privileged to share it who lingered long after class before returning to East Harlem (in my case) or the outer boroughs. That cohort and those to follow owe much gratitude to the unsung heroine Melissa Hammerle, whose efforts at New York University should earn her at least a century's worth of acknowledgment in American letters. Being awed by the company of great names, however, faded quickly.

I studied with Breyten Breytenbach and Kimiko Hahn; Yusef Komunyakaa and Sharon Olds; Phillis Levin, Phil Levine, and Anne Carson, but a great poet does not a great teacher make. The worst of them simply tried too hard, assigning pitiful texts they either thought would be useful, based on the abstract printed in an academic press catalog, or wished for during their juvenescence, when becoming a poet required only adept reading comprehension, an autodidact's determination, and no degree. One poet's craft class was so inadequate that a few of my peers asked me to facilitate a Saturday morning workshop on prosody. I had studied with Marilyn Hacker at a public institution uptown and they wanted to know what she had taught me. I turned them down and advised them to complain to the new director of the program. Other poets did not even try to pretend they knew what they were doing and made it up as they went along. One was a bona fide genius: a true scholar and born educator. She had the answers but it was graduate school, and everyone was afraid to admit that they had no idea what a *teleuton* was. The best of them offered what in their opinion were great poems and helped us out of the muck we brought in on a Monday night. This did more than any anthology of received forms could have done because it illuminated the teaching poet's own foundation and helped me visualize the trajectory of where she or he thought strong poetry was going.

Phil Levine was safely in this latter group. To be honest, I had never read any of his work but certainly knew who he was. I had heard stories, mostly about his humor in the classroom and penchant for red wine. As most of my cohort did with our other professors, I read all of his work several weeks before my first class with him. Phil is a strong poet, possessing a genuine passion for poetry as an art form, a High Romantic aesthetic buried beneath that midwestern working-man braggadocio and a vast amount of twentieth-century American poetry at his beck and call—and that was him at seventy-eight, in khaki pants and running shoes! From his work, I understood that he understood people. His poetry never attempts to mask our base motivations and neither did his teaching.

As an MFA student, I had a reputation for being arrogant, and, as my publisher told me during our first editorial meeting a few months after I left the university, one of my peers had berated me at a literary soirée as the "pompous Negro." Too true, I am afraid. When I began the program I was coming down from the high of being the first person in my immediate family to go to college, let alone graduate and go on to more advanced studies—the child of a teenaged single mother. I had a fellowship, not a basketball scholarship. I was engaged in a noncommercial discipline with no lucrative prospects. My story is not new. For me, Poetry was and is a serious endeavor. I did not enroll because I wanted to be the next Robert Creeley or because being a successful lawyer was not in the cards, or because I lusted after Marie Howe and might stumble across her in the hall and become entangled. I did not seek Poetry, nor did It find me to heal my past. In fact, the moment anyone started crying in a workshop was an opportunity for me to take a bathroom break. I did not have time for any bullshit.

Phil recognized this immediately. Perhaps it was a telepathic recognition of sorts. We are both Capricorns, fifty-two years and three days apart in age. I never used the word *bullshit* in speech until after I met Phil. Besides humor and red wine, he had a penchant for cussing, and never did an offensive word sound sweeter than coming from Phil's mouth. One night in his workshop, a peer submitted some raggedy poem for critique about a dream and a bevy of fantasy women. As usual, I jumped in first and said, "This is bullshit!" I was not offering "The Second Coming" that night, but what was before us *was* bullshit. Phil laughed aloud. The peer in question knew it was bullshit. I was not made to apologize. No other critique was necessary. We moved on to the next poem. Any other professor would have asked me to leave, reiterate workshop etiquette, or at least made me apologize. Not Phil.

The man constantly regaled us with stories about Lowell and Berryman and Spain under Franco. He knew the agon intimately and how important it was for emerging poets to be aware of it, to identify it—as we had already taken up the mantle. The strongest poet in my cohort was Ishion Hutchinson. Twenty-four years old and fresh from Jamaica, his poems obliterated anything anyone else turned in. He was the real deal, even as a student. Think Derek Walcott and Shaka Zulu collided, sailing up a floodplain river in an attempt to take Bobo Hill, with an incantation composed in terza rima. He would starve and deprive himself of sleep until the final line came. Phil knew this and we talked about it. He said, "Ishion is feeling out so many ways to go about a poem . . . There is this wonderful variety of structure, tone, voice, subject . . . you turn the page not knowing who or what will be there." Phil did not take my part in the conversation as a cry for help or his part as pastoral solution. Established poets, especially those who teach, are more than willing to give examples of good poems and explain why they are good. I always make it a point to ask poets I admire for examples of bad poems and explanations of why they are bad. They stumble over the answer or refuse to offer one, not seeing the point of the question, its value. Phil is the only exception. It was because of his honesty, his fearless striding through the field hacking down the weeds to fortify the crop, that I learned discernment—of image, of line, of poem. I learned to not be intimidated by strong poetry but to breach it, via whatever route was accessible.

The end of my semester with Phil fell just shy of his seventy-ninth birthday, and, according to him, our class was to be his last. We agreed we had to do something memorable, a cherry to top all the sweet memories that would fill his *retirement*—whatever that means for a poet. On December 11, 2007, we assembled on the second floor of the townhouse in what I like to call the Thesis Room (not our usual meeting space), because the walls were lined with bookshelves containing, behind paned doors, the theses of alumni. To celebrate the last class we crowded the table with baked goods, candy canes, plastic cups, Rioja, poems, and a horrendous-looking, store-bought cake. To celebrate Phil's birthday, however, was a brand-spanking-new home video game console called a Wii. One could play tennis on it, which someone had heard Phil liked to do. It was a magnificent night. We drank, read poems, and watched Phil attack the game with a child's enthusiasm and a Capricorn's determination. There was a freestyle rap session. For some reason, the great Ishion Hutchinson and the dreamy Zachary Sussman ended up with their shirts off!

As much revelry as was had that night, it could not compare to the near sublime and fondest memory I keep of Phil. Two or three weeks before our festivities, we were having a rather ordinary workshop. Phil usually had an anecdote from the weekend or earlier day, which would lead him to some recollection about Fresno or line by César Vallejo and then we would get down to business. Yet, this night he somehow got onto William Carlos Williams and, for a few moments, was completely gripped by "The Sparrow." He leaned over the table, his eyes glossy with remembering, and began a recitation. Silence. The awe of being in the company of a great name again. The agon, visible and pulsating. In hindsight, those lines were Phil's ultimate lesson:

Practical to the end,
            it is the poem
                        of his existence
        that triumphed
            finally;
                        a wisp of feathers
        flattened to the pavement,
            wings spread symmetrically
                        as if in flight,
        the head gone,
            the black escutcheon of the breast
                        undecipherable,

an effigy of a sparrow,
        a dried wafer only,
                left to say
and it says it
        without offense,
                beautifully;
This was I,
        a sparrow.
                I did my best;
farewell.

The Simple Voice of Philip Levine

TOMÁS Q. MORÍN

In the fall of 1998, with an undergraduate Spanish degree in my pocket, I began my first semester in the PhD program at Johns Hopkins University. If everything went according to plan, five years of studying and dissecting the writers I revered would have me walking in a polyester robe to "Pomp and Circumstance," a new soldier in the ranks of critics. Everything, however, didn't go according to plan. While my teachers and classmates were kind and welcoming, I was a twenty-two-year-old kid who, before that year, had never left Texas. I was miserable. Baltimore offered little solace; the city was withdrawn and surly. Wallace Stevens could've been describing it when he famously wrote "The world is ugly / and the people are sad." What I didn't yet know that summer, as my future wife and I loaded a U-Haul and began the long drive to Maryland, was that most of my life I'd lived with dysthymia, a constant, low-level depression. In Baltimore, homesick and lonely, I found myself desperately seeking things to make me happy. Movies, exercising, and socializing had failed to cheer me up, but reading and writing poetry became a balm.

In the lower levels of the university's Eisenhower Library, I encountered the poets who would sustain me. The nights I should've been repairing the glaring gaps in my knowledge of French Deconstructionism, I instead spent catching up on American poetry written during the sixties, seventies, and eighties. I devoured books like Donald Justice's *The Summer Anniversaries*, Anthony Hecht's *The Hard Hours*, Charles Wright's *China Trace*, and W. S. Merwin's *The Drunk in the Furnace* as if they were medicine. Whenever my department offered a seminar on Walt Whitman or Pablo Neruda, I found a small haven where I could talk freely about American poetry without fear of betraying my new passion.

One of the other programs that shared the building with my department was the famed Writing Seminars. On more than one occasion, I found myself wandering on their floor looking for God knows what. If a poetry teacher or a student had engaged me in conversation, I don't know what I would have said. My guess is, nothing. If at that moment I had possessed the vision to see that writing would one day become my vocation, I would have lacked the courage to share that with anyone.

During one of my clandestine visits to the poetry stacks, the chocolate spine and bright lettering of a tall, thin volume caught my eye. The book was *1933* by Philip Levine. Standing there, I read one poem, and then another and another. The strong, intimate voice, the spare images of family and loss, and the movement of the poems down and across the page entranced me. I didn't need to know iambs or syllabics to appreciate the rhythms, to feel them in my pulse.

The music of Phil's poems was the first revelation; the second was his people. As I flipped through more of his books, I encountered barbers, children, factory workers, musicians, and anarchists. These people were never abstractions; they were characters whose joys and pains, triumphs and defeats were chronicled with a crystalline vision. In poem after poem, he cast the lives from his working-class roots with dignity and affection.

This isn't to say that the characters in his poems were completely autobiographical. All one had to do was read the poems about his sisters who didn't exist or the one about his birth in Lucerne to realize that, in his hands, poems were more than just personal confessions.

The next few happy months of reading and writing were electrifying. My imagination popped and sparked. The only interruption came the week I hung over my bed a dream catcher that my mother had sent me. Instead of catching my nightmares, it seemed to cause me to dream constantly—something I rarely do. During the day, however, my imagination was dead. I was miserable. The first morning after I'd tossed it in the trash, I wrote a poem. The sense of relief and joy I felt forced me to recognize the obvious: poetry had replaced my passion for scholarship. My problem was that I didn't know whether I had any potential, at least not enough to warrant abandoning my doctoral program for an MFA.

By this time, I'd confided in one of my classmates from Spain about my double life. Knowing how much I loved Phil's work, she suggested I write to him and ask for his opinion. I was shocked by her suggestion and quickly dismissed it. It didn't seem possible that someone could just write to Philip Levine, much less solicit his advice. I remember thinking: maybe in her home country ordinary people write to their poetry gods—their Lorcas and Machados and Albertís—all the time. But not here. Not in Baltimore.

A few weeks later, in a moment of desperation, I shed my reticence and dashed off a letter to Phil in which I explained my circumstances and asked whether he would be willing to look at a few poems and tell me if he thought there was anything worth pursuing. After I mailed the letter, I immediately regretted it and wished I could take it back, but it was too late.

Weeks passed and I all but forgot my moment of temporary insanity. The possibility that my letter had been lost or misplaced by some overworked intern at his publisher Knopf brought me comfort. But one afternoon, I reached into my mailbox and found an envelope from Fresno. Thinking I'd find a polite, apologetic note about why a famous and busy writer couldn't help me, I wasn't prepared for what Phil had actually written: an invitation to send him a few poems I had faith in. Filled with excitement and fear, I sent him three poems. I had to wait only ten days for his response.

In his wiry handwriting, Phil explained how in one overwrought poem about my grandfather's hands, I'd betrayed my ignorance of how blood flows through the human body. I'd also been careless with antecedents and indulged in vague language. Phil had written "BS" next to more than a dozen lines where, according to him, I had "let [my] intelligence fall asleep." In his letter, he wrote, "As I recall, you wanted to know if you should pursue a career in poetry. I don't know why you would ask. If you don't *have to* write poetry, do something else. One poem suggests a real talent. All three suggest you don't know a hell of a lot about writing poems." He then said, in the world of poetry "the rewards are small unless the reward of writing is *enormous.*"

My mind was made up. I *had* to write poetry. Before Phil's letter, I had felt adrift, but now I had a direction. With my wife's support and encouragement, I decided to leave the security of Johns Hopkins. In the summer of 2000 we packed our things and trekked back to Texas, where I enrolled in the MFA program at Texas State University. A few years went by and I had no further contact with Phil until my final semester, when I chose his name from the program's list of outside thesis readers. I'd been warned that Phil had a reputation for being hard on the work of students, especially graduate students. In spite of these warnings, I put together the best thesis I could and sent it to him, hoping I would show him how much I'd learned in the three years since he'd read my three poems.

What I received in return was a three-page, single-spaced letter explaining the comments, written in his usual brown ink, that peppered my thesis. Phil opened his letter to me by saying that the poems in my thesis were lazy, propped up by an "orphic" voice reliant on a stable of words repeated endlessly, what he called "my old tried and untrue vocabulary." He recommended I read Aristotle's *Poetics* because it was obvious I had "no awareness of the unities of time, place, and action."

As I reviewed his notes, I discovered Phil had scribbled "rescue" at least as many times as "bullshit." It was clear he wanted me to throw my poems a life preserver, to save the emotions and ideas from which they had come by "taking a hard look at what rolls easily onto the page." In short, grad school had taught me about making images, a voice, a musical line, but instead of bringing these elements together in the staging of a poem, I was simply using each one to flood the page with language and call it poetry. He didn't mince words when he told me I'd pissed him off by treating my poems so poorly.

At the end of his letter, Phil wrote that his teacher, John Berryman, had pushed him to be tough on his poems: "I did not take him as seriously as I should have, & many of the poems in my books should have been better. I had the skill to make them better & I settled for less."

To say I was dumbstruck is an understatement. While I couldn't imagine what poems he could be referring to—I still can't—I was no less humbled by his revelation. Here was the winner of every poetry award under the sun sharing with me that he'd failed some of his own poems and that he didn't want me to repeat his mistakes. The fact that he treated my poems as if they were his own spoke volumes to his generosity as a teacher.

After a few days of licking my wounds, I wrote to Phil to thank him for his generous advice and the attention he'd given my work. In the following year,

I wrote to him about the challenges of life after graduation, always including some poems in which I tried to apply the lessons he'd offered. His positive responses and continued encouragement let me know he was excited about the worlds I was creating in my poems, as well as the odd cast of characters that populated them.

Before long, if I sent him a poem with a letter, he wouldn't mention the poem in his reply. Whether wrongly or rightly, I took his silence about the poems as a gentle nudge that he couldn't be my teacher forever. From then on, we happily exchanged letters about jazz and the blues, our love of boxing and Hemingway, the challenges of teaching, and the harsh realities of the poetry business.

Though a dozen years have passed since Phil answered my first plea, it's impossible for me to measure his impact on my life. We've spoken in person only a handful of times, but his words are never far from me. As I struggled to write the ending to this essay, Phil's lessons were there to help. Even though I tried my best to compare the sound of Phil's voice to a morning bell calling me to work or a horn leading me safely through fog or something else both noble and beautiful, when I need him most, I hear none of these things. Instead, I hear the word *bullshit* in Phil's sweet baritone, a voice that always seems on the verge of breaking into laughter. And then his voice says to me, *Be tough* and *Tell it straight*. And so I have.

High above the Atlantic

MALENA MÖRLING

Certain people have appeared in my life as if they were angels. They have always arrived at times when it was critical for me to turn a corner or to navigate a particularly difficult stretch of road in order to travel on toward more fruitful and rewarding experiences. When I look back at the events that make up my life, it is clear to me how these people have been important in ways that might be impossible to explain in words. And when I imagine what my life would have been like without them, it all goes dark, becomes a lost life, a life devoid of entire realms of beauty, sanity, humor, courage, and common sense.

Philip Levine is one of these people: a cornerstone in my development as a writer, a person from whom I have learned everything that is important in regards to living a life trying to write poems. He was a great teacher, primarily because he taught by example, by being totally and unequivocally himself. Levine did not come to class armed with a stack of quirky exercises or assignments for us to complete; he never had a prefabricated topic in mind for discussion, nor did he ever have us write in particular, prescribed forms, such as sonnets or sestinas. It was not that he believed formal poems should not be written, for some of the students in the class wrote in given forms, and that, I think, delighted him. It was more that he believed we ought to write directly out of the experience of who we were and out of the moment of the poem as it was occurring. He often stressed that if one lets one's rational mind or intelligence take over, or if one stays with what one initially thought to write before embarking on the actual writing, it is impossible to write an original poem. It is also impossible to evolve as a writer this way because in order to evolve or grow, the writer must follow the imagination of the poem to new and undiscovered territory. In other words, in order not to write a poem that has already been written, the writer must trust and follow the imagination. It is the most important thing of all. I can still hear him say: *The poem is smarter than you are!* Therefore, it did not behoove Levine to give us any assignment other than to bring a new poem to every class.

Thus Levine arrived to class empty handed, carrying only a small yellow knapsack across one shoulder. He always entered the classroom slowly, as if he had all the time in the world. In fact, I have never seen him rush anywhere or lose his calm and sane presence, even in New York City, where everyone else is rushing down the sidewalks as if they are perpetually late for something important. Even there, Levine walked slowly. When I was a graduate student in the Creative Writing Program at New York University in 1991, I sometimes saw him before class strolling along University Place as if he had made a promise to life never to rush through it, but instead to carry himself steadily, with clarity and dignity, always noticing what was occurring around him. After he settled into a chair in the classroom, we'd give him our freshly written poems and he'd allow the moment to dictate what would happen next.

In class after class, Levine's teaching was ingenious and effortless; he never had to reach far to get to the problem with one of our poems or to point out its strengths. He was outrageously honest and had a way of making us all laugh, even at ourselves, which proved invaluable, given that most of the time the poems we brought to class were not yet poems. He shot down bullshit quickly and did not allow us to make excuses for our poems, or for anything. He encouraged us to keep on working on our poems, to revise them, and to bring revisions to him during his office hours. Often, a long line of students would be waiting outside his office, but no matter how many people were there to see him, he never appeared distracted or rushed in a meeting. He'd calmly read my poem, giving it his full and undivided attention.

Before I met Levine, I found his poems at Shakespeare & Co. on the Upper West Side of Manhattan. On a shelf that housed many of his books, I was drawn in particular to *1933*. I was struck by the voice of the poems, a voice whose strength was unmistakable and whose lyricism was at once deeply rooted and tender. At that time, I had mostly read T. S. Eliot; I owned his *Selected Poems* and carried it with me everywhere. I had also read Sylvia Plath's *Ariel* and I was a bit infatuated with the mellifluous voice of Hart Crane, even though I often did not understand his poems. Also, some months before, a friend had lent me a copy of the *Complete Poems of Wallace Stevens* and urged me to read "The Man with the Blue Guitar." But nothing I had read had prepared me for the clarity and the engaging rhythm of Levine's poems, which were about life the way it really is, without needless embellishments. I noticed, too, how the lucidity of the poems was tinged with a surrealism that helped reveal the beauty and mystery of that which is common, that which one might even dismiss as ugly. I also saw how his poems were about real people with real, ordinary lives. And the poems held within them an industrial landscape, and they often illuminated unremarkable human situations and places that hardly anyone notices because they are so obvious that we take them for granted, as we do our own forgotten breaths. Of course, *1933* is a book very much about loss: in 1933 Levine's father died when Levine was only five years old, and the book is, in a sense, an elegy for his family. I somehow made a connection then, emotionally and somewhat abstractly, with those poems, perhaps because I had, only a few years before, left Sweden for the United States, and I had lost nearly everything and everyone in my former life. Perhaps I recognized something in Levine's poems of my own unremarkable, ordinary life and family, as well as something of the rather dull and orderly industrial harbor town in which I had grown up.

Maybe a year after finding Levine's poems, while traveling back to the United States after a visit to family and friends in Sweden, I was reading *1933* for the umpteenth time and began to hear the poems in my head in Swedish. High above the Atlantic Ocean, I scribbled down the first drafts of my translations of the poems into Swedish. That fall, I had the great fortune to meet Levine after a magnificent and hilarious poetry reading he gave at the University of Massachusetts in Amherst, where I was living and studying. After his reading I was awestruck and a little nervous, but I walked up to him and told him that I was translating his poems into Swedish. Upon hearing this, he appeared delighted, and his friendly demeanor put me immediately at ease.

After that, I wrote Levine a letter thanking him for the reading and told him that I had questions about some of the poems I was translating; could we meet sometime? I believe I also sent him a few of my poems. I received a generous and encouraging letter in answer inviting me to meet with him during his office hours at Tufts University.

As I sat opposite Levine in his modest, nondescript office, I was most struck by his kind and earnest face and his lively yet grounded presence. There was something unusually sane and fun and accepting about him. For one, he was incredibly generous and patient with my list of questions. I had never before translated anything and was still finding my way in English. I worried that my questions would make him wonder what was going to come of this translation project. Yet he kindly answered every one of them, even engaging me with stories of events that had inspired the poems. Over the years he has been extraordinarily patient with my translations of his poems. I published some of them in literary magazines, but it was not until the summer of 2011 that *1933* finally came out in Sweden, just before Levine was appointed United States Poet Laureate.

During that meeting with him, he not only answered my translation questions, he also asked me about my own writing and what I was currently reading. I was reading Wordsworth and Coleridge and taking a class on the Lake Poets. This excited him because he had recently been rereading Wordsworth and said that he appreciated him more now in middle age than when he had been younger. After we talked a while, he had to go teach his Introduction to Poetry Class and invited me along. I was so lucky at that moment and I must have known it, for the incredible experience of studying with Levine—for one semester as an undergraduate at Tufts and for another as a graduate student at NYU—was still ahead of me.

Writing this, I am reminded of what Larry Levis, Levine's student and close friend, wrote in his brilliant essay about him:

> He is the only person I have ever known who seemed to be fully awake to this life, his own and the lives of others. An amazing talker, it surprised me when I noticed how deeply and closely he listened to students . . .
>
> Why in the world did he care so much about what we did? Because we mattered so much to him, we began to matter to ourselves. And to matter in this way, to feel that what one did and how one wrote actually might make a difference, was a crucial gift Levine gave to each of us.

I know this gift from Levine helped save me from myself and empowered and inspired me to pursue, no matter how impossible or impractical, a life trying to write poems. I can't think of anything more valuable and beautiful than a gift such as this, with its indelible and resonant presence.

A Love Supreme

Notes toward an Appropriate Gratitude

JOHN MURILLO

1

I can't lie. That August afternoon, when I heard that my teacher had been ap-
pointed United States Poet Laureate, I felt the way one does upon hearing any
big news concerning a loved one. Proud. You know what pride is. If you're old
enough to read this, you know what pride is. Your mother gets a long overdue
promotion at her job. Your big brother knocks out the neighborhood bully.
Your friend Calvin owns his own McDonalds. Call it cool by proxy, residual
props. Put simply: they win, you win. As if their successes and the work put
into achieving those successes have anything under the stars to do with you.
Of course, they don't. And this didn't.

Still. Here is someone who's devoted his whole life to poetry, without much
concern for accolades, receiving what is arguably the highest honor that can be
given an American poet. And he didn't do it by schmoozing and glad-handing.
He didn't get it because of his pedigree or connects (Phil's never been that guy).
He earned it simply on the merits of his work and what it's come to mean to
American letters. In so doing, he confirmed for me everything he's ever tried
to teach his students about maintaining one's personal and artistic integrity.
So on that muggy Brooklyn afternoon—because I knew Phil was a little too
grounded to make much of a fuss about any of it himself, and because I felt

someone somewhere needed to—I did a little dance, kissed my lady hard on the mouth, and poured us two cool glasses of something sweet.

This was just a day or two before I left to attend the Bread Loaf Writers' Conference in Vermont. Phil was one of the scheduled guests and, with news of his appointment fresh in the air, the excitement surrounding his visit was palpable. I was looking forward to seeing him, of course. It had been a few months since the last time, and I can always count on him to say something that I know will have me either cracking up, walking a bit taller, or both.

About a week into the conference—the night before Phil was to give his reading—the novelist Richard Bausch kidnapped some of us fellows and forced us to miss out on the cafeteria fare in order to enjoy steak and fine wine at a nearby restaurant. We had been seated only a few minutes when Phil walked in with his wife, Franny, and some other family members and friends. Seated next to me was one of those writers who always has to let you know how well connected he is, who he knows, how far they go back, etc. So when he noticed how excited I was to see Phil, he nudged me, "Hey, you know who that is?" Before I could answer, he continued, "it's Philip Levine. We met once, I wonder if he will remember me?" When Phil approached our table, Bausch stood to shake his hand and announced to the group: "Ladies and gentlemen, may I have your attention, please? I'd like to introduce you all to the recently appointed Poet Laureate of the United States, Philip Levine!" Then, spotting me at the other end of the table, and without missing a beat, Phil cut into the applause, "And ladies and gentlemen, I'd like to introduce you to one of the best students I've ever had . . . John Murillo!" Then, "So everything he knows," tipping an invisible hat, "he owes to someone else!" I leaned over to Mr. Connected: "You know, I thought he looked familiar but I wasn't sure."

I love Phil. Now, suddenly I can't stand the love flooding me for Phil.

2

I first met Phil in the fall of 2005. That was the year I decided to pack a U-Haul with everything I owned, leave behind my job and everyone I knew, and try to start a life in New York City. There, I would live on a fraction of what I earned as a third-grade teacher in Washington, D.C., and spend my days reading and writing poems. I had decided to go back to school. Not law school, or medical school, but poetry school. I was thirty-four years old.

I couldn't explain this decision to anyone around me in a way that would make sense. It was just something I had to do. I had been writing and work-shopping with a talented group of D.C. poets who taught me much about craft (shouts to Brandon, Renegade, Sami, and Nesto!), but I needed more. If I was to reach my potential as a poet, I knew I had to throw myself into it with everything I had. This wasn't a game to me, wasn't a hobby.

If I had any doubts whether I had made the best move, Phil shut them down right away. I believe it was during one of our first class meetings when—in response, I think, to a student who may have been misquoting Dana Gioia—Phil leaned forward, seeming to look each of us in the eyes at the same time, "There is nothing—nothing!—more important than what you're doing right here." I don't think I have ever heard anyone, before or since, speak about her or his life's work with as much conviction as Phil showed us that evening. And he was not bullshitting. Nearing his eightieth birthday and still believing the way he did . . . how could anyone in his presence not want to live for this? If I had not attended another single session with Phil, what he gave me in that moment, in that tiny room, would have been worth the move. A single sentence uttered with so much soul that, years later, I still live by it.

And this, I believe, is Phil's greatest gift as a teacher: he believes in poetry, period. Not in poetry as a means to some political, spiritual, or financial end—though it can be, and often is, one or more of these things to many people—but as something good and worthwhile in and of itself. And because he believes in poetry so completely, he demands from his students that they either honor it, or leave it the hell alone. As he and his own classmates used to say about John Berryman's workshop at Iowa, "This thing with the poems is serious."

3

Years ago I studied Kung Fu. I learned that the term *Kung Fu* refers not to the fighting art, per se, but to a mastery of self and circumstance, achieved through the dedicated practice of that art. Kung Fu, then, can be realized and expressed by various means, if practiced in earnest. If achieved in any one area, it can carry over into other aspects of one's life.

I consider this the big take-away from Phil's teaching. To dedicate oneself wholly—to whatever it is one is into—is the only way to live. If you're going to do something, do it. And if one thing is as good as another (which Phil never said, truth be told), then no pursuit is necessarily either more or less valuable than another. What matters is *how* we pursue. Phil, like his own Berryman before him, would have us attack with everything we have and are. Every poem, each line. Excellence at every turn.

He modeled this for us in the ways that mattered most. He took his work as a teacher as seriously as he did his work as a poet. He never phoned it in and never allowed his students to either.

One night, because the teaching assistants at New York University were striking and Phil refused to break the picket line, we held class in the apartment of one of the students. (Any other teacher would have taken this as an opportunity to cancel class. But like I say, Phil wasn't any other teacher.) At the time, I didn't feel like my poems were being read with the same rigor as those of the other students. So that night I brought in a deliberately bad poem—a villanelle about a pimp named Willie and his main woman, Moonglow—to see whether anyone would say anything. As I predicted, my classmates put on the kid gloves and complimented me on punctuation and grammar, and of course the poem's musicality. Many thought it was praiseworthy that I would even try to write a villanelle (which reminded me of comedian Chris Rock's skit about the backhanded compliments some white would-be voters gave Colin Powell when considering him as a presidential candidate: "He speaks so well!" To which Rock responded: "He's a fucking educated man! How the hell is he supposed to sound?!"). This went on for about four minutes before Phil broke in and called me out. "John," he said, "we've already heard this story a million times; the story about the black pimp and his whore. Don't blacks get enough of this kind of treatment on TV and in the movies without you caricaturing them, too? C'mon, John. You're a better writer than this." The class was stunned silent. But they recovered soon enough, seeing that I didn't fall to pieces or flip the table or produce an Uzi from my book bag. And after that, I got the same hard treatment as anyone else. The rest of the workshop went very well. And I gained even more respect for Phil that night, knowing I could always count on him to be honest with me, to always give it to me straight, no chaser.

4

I was in Phil's workshop for only a semester (just as he himself studied only a few weeks with his own great mentor, Berryman), but he's been my teacher for years. What he taught and continues to teach me is primarily by example.

To watch Philip Levine move through the world is to be given the rare opportunity to learn what it means to live with conviction and integrity. To have spent even a little time with him is to learn from someone who knows the meaning of honor and grace.

Many of Phil's more recent students, including myself, are at a strange crossroads in our writing lives. We're at that point where such concerns as publishing and gaining employment, trying to make a way in the literary world, can easily distract from why we came to poetry in the first place. What some people call the "Po-Biz" is leading many of us to develop attitudes and act in ways we otherwise wouldn't. Some of us will publish books we know aren't worth a damn because we want to speed along the tenure process. Others will dine with people we don't respect because they chair this board or that. A few of us may write positive reviews for books we don't like, hoping for a kickback somewhere down the line. We'll know it's all bullshit, but we'll do it anyway. We'll make excuses for ourselves, and over time it will become easier and easier to sell ourselves out. But in those quiet moments—after the checks have been cashed, the books signed and sold—when we're sitting with ourselves, our teacher will come to us. And if we can still ourselves just a bit, we'll be able to hear that rough voice urging us to be better than we've been. "There is nothing—nothing!—more important than what you're doing right here." If we quiet ourselves, and maybe shut out all that other noise, we can hear Phil, like a favorite tune that always calls us back to ourselves.

An Apprentice's Tale

DANIEL NESTER

When was the first time I saw Philip Levine? I'm pretty sure it was the first day of classes at New York University in the fall of 1995, out in the lounge with ratty couches, on the second floor of 19 University Place. He sat next to Gerald Stern. They talked about the food in New York and the great poets of Cleveland. Who? Hart Crane and . . . where in Ohio is Rita Dove from? Some of us joined naming names. Who else? d. a. levy? Yes, d. a. levy, I threw in his name. The desire to impress fogs my memory. Later, Levine, dressed in a sweater and collared shirt, nice jacket, sat at the end of the seminar table as we walked in.

I had been in the city for a year, had committed to making something of myself as a poet, and assumed Levine and I would be simpatico, fellow blue-collar travelers. I even might have thought that I had "outgrown" Levine's poems, fancying myself a more experimental type. The sequence of different disguises I wore in those days is still unclear.

What is clear is that I was at once worshipful and ambivalent about being in the same room as the poet who redefined, for me, what was acceptable subject matter in a contemporary poem and how to go about writing about work. Here I was, twenty-six, old by grad student standards, with this sixty-seven-year-old poet, in the flesh, about to read our poems for the next fifteen weeks.

I do remember the first time I read Levine's poems. It was the fall of 1991, my first poetry workshop, led by Michael S. Weaver (now Afaa M. Weaver) at Rutgers University in Camden, New Jersey. I was a nonmatriculated student who had limped through undergrad. We're talking figuratively, but I also wore a polio brace on my right leg from a landscaping job accident. The figure I struck then was Dickensian. My leg clacked as I walked.

Weaver assigned several poets who remain favorites—Li-Young Lee, Sharon Olds—but the one who stood out for me was Philip Levine. You know the poem:

> You know what work is—if you're
> old enough to read this you know what
> work is, although you may not do it.

His poems woke me up because I knew what work was. My grandfather, Curt Little, worked twenty years at a printer where he cut holes through green Turnpike tickets. When the owner went out of business, my grandfather lost his pension. I never heard him complain. My father, Mike Nester, worked nights as a truck driver, dead-lifted forty-pound boxes off the docks, rolled metal drums onto forklifts. My sister walked on his back, cracking vertebrae into place. Through high school, I worked at a car wash, where I scrubbed whitewalls with wire brushes and dried off bumpers. I didn't have proper work boots or gloves. I put plastic bags over my sneakers with rubber bands.

Philip Levine introduced the idea to me that blue-collar work is worthy of being made into a poem, of being poetic. Poetry was no longer just a rich person's game. And so when Afaa Weaver, who worked in a factory for fifteen years before entering the world of poetry, asked me, "What are you going to do with all these poems?," it changed my world. I sat up straight. He suggested this absurd thing called creative writing school.

As long as I can remember, I've had a conflicted relationship with the word *mentor*. It suggests to me a patrilineal passing of the torch or priestly rite of worship. I'm sure this started for me when poetry took the place of faith in God. I was about nineteen, and it was a welcome change. Still, I was skeptical of poetry. I wasn't ready, to paraphrase T. S. Eliot, to "surrender wholly to the work."

Back then I was a nervous wretch, in most ways unmentorable; I was outgoing and social, but also insecure and rude and still hurting from a father who left the family. If I wasn't writing poems about empty driveways and union jackets left on the hanger, I was writing about nosehair-picking. There was no time to be genteel; a poem had to reflect the brute significance of the oppressed reality of the human spirit, what William Carlos Williams calls the "human particulars." My particulars didn't involve paintings, animals, or allusions to philosophy, which seemed to appear in every poem I read in literary journals. I'm tired just explaining it to you now, but back then, that was the credo.

I was needy. Sometimes, it was all I could do to blurt out, all at once, my life story, so that Levine understood me completely, knew completely why I was sitting in that chair, in that room, with these poems, with him. That temptation to confess sat at the tip of my tongue, lapsed Catholic that I was. At other times, I assumed he'd divine I was part of his blue-collar tribe, that we shared this common drudgery.

The assumptions varied, but it became evident that Levine just wanted to read and discuss our poems. He was going to read poems, mark them with a pencil, underline words, cross out others. And that, to me, is where the real mentorship began.

That first class, Levine addressed a rumor about his teaching methods. "You might've heard," he said, "some story where I tore up somebody's poem in front of everybody, and this made many people upset, including the writer of that poem. That's not true."

I'd heard the story, as had everyone else, and we were surprised he met the story head-on. We knew Levine was a tough customer, or at least had a different communication style, from, say, Sharon Olds, who maintained a yogic calm as we picked each other's poems apart. I think some of us would have worn it like a badge of honor if Levine tore up one of our poems; I know I would have.

It wasn't all kumbaya. Levine did confront us in class. "What was the greatest book of 'New York poetry' ever written?" he asked us one night. A pause hung in the air. My friend Christopher Connelly sat across the table from me. He said one word under his breath—"Lorca?"—so low it sounded like a cough.

"What was that?" Levine asked. "Did someone say Lorca?"

Connelly later said he thought he was wrong and should take back what he said. And just when he was about to, Levine pounced. "Right!" he said. "You are absolutely right. Federico García Lorca's *Poet in New York*."

This was a rare moment when someone got the right answer, or had any answer. A class with Philip Levine was more about finding the questions to ask.

Levine said he liked teaching at NYU because we "didn't act like we were the anointed." This was true. Our group of twelve was serious about work and we gave each other, as we say, great feedback, as great as any class I'd been in, before or since. There were no alliances or payback pools, all of which I've seen and some of which I've participated in.

We were also not very sophisticated in the ways of the Po-Biz. In the years after NYU, I wished we'd been debriefed in navigating the confidence games every poet must play. I may sound like an old man who walked barefoot uphill to school, but back in our day, our program didn't have much in the way of career advice besides a stack of *Writer's Chronicles* and a bulletin board announcing crappy contests. Writing programs are more adept at faking these things now.

In recent years I have come to think it is good we focused on our poems and poetry in that room. It was a far more pure process, for one, to see our professor take each line of ours, pencil in hand, and match each individual talent to a tradition. Besides, what were we going to do—ask Philip Fucking Levine about what to say in a cover letter or how many poems to send with a SASE to *Kenyon Review*?

I am looking at a WordPerfect file of poems I wrote that semester: forty-seven poems, along with forty drafts of others. One, "Parade," a stanza-by-stanza imitation of Robert Lowell's "Skunk Hour," swaps Fats Domino's "Careless Love" with Journey's power ballad "Open Arms" and ends with oversexed MTV videos instead of a family of skunks.

Another poem is so shamelessly imitative of Levine's I dare not mention its title, only that it involves chalk, an homage to his "The Poem of Chalk," and frying potatoes, an allusion to his "The Simple Truth." I know I was not the only one who cribbed words and allusions to spark up an interest in the old man. Imagine collecting these derivative poems from these souls week after week! Imagine the reticence required not to say: *Knock it off, brown-noser. Stop imitating me, and write your own damn poems.*

It is not uncommon for poets to send work to teachers after the semester is over, to keep in touch. It doesn't make sense now, but back then I made a conscious decision not to do this. Levine offered me encouragement and direction, some direct advice. We talked about William Carlos Williams, about "Asphodel, That Greeny Flower" and marriage.

I never attempted to keep up a correspondence with Levine. I don't think he would have wanted to, but that's not the point. I'm not sure what such a correspondence would have consisted of. Would I have kept on sending him poems, and he'd offer mild encouragement? It didn't make sense, at least to me, to do such a thing, and to be honest, I saw it as kissing up or striving. Other people don't feel that way, I know, but back then, that's how it felt. There were people who bragged about "still talking" to their old teachers. Or maybe they weren't bragging. Maybe these things simply happen. Regardless, my thought on this matter was always, and still is: Why bother them?

I worked as a secretary at NYU after graduate school, and occasionally I would see Levine in the gym locker room. There he was, Philip Levine, taking off his pants or putting his towel in a gym bag. I think he swam. I did say hello to him once. It was awkward. We were both half-naked. He was nice, but I don't think he remembered me, or remembered me in the way I would have wanted him to, which would have been as some poetic genius. It didn't matter. We had spent our time together, and that time was over. I read his poems, he read mine, and then we got back to work doing what we did before.

Although I have had many excellent teachers in my lifetime, I never thought I had enjoyed the benefits of having a mentor. My thoughts on these matters have changed. Maybe it's because I am now a father twice over. Maybe I've gotten soft in middle age. What I've learned is it's best to acknowledge one's mentors, and, two decades later, that's better than not doing anything at all. I look back with a terrible regret for not being open to having mentors or acknowledging them. I think of Afaa Weaver, my first mentor, as well as Philip Levine, because of their work backgrounds, sure; but also, frankly, they take on a paternal glow in my rearview mirror. They feel like my fathers.

I think back to years beneath that goddamn car wash blower, how I could scream along with it and no one could hear me. How it's muffled my hearing to this day. Whenever I shift one foot to another, I know I don't have to limp around anymore. I can stand straight up.

Reading Philip Levine in 1972

SHARON OLDS

When I first read the poems of Philip Levine, I knew I was in the presence of something brand new and very important. I hadn't read anything like them before. (I was maybe about thirty years old, a wife and mother, living in New York City, who had grown up in California, written a lot of stories and poems as a child and a teenager, and was now finishing—with a lot of difficulty—a graduate degree in literature.) His poems sparkled and crackled with passionate conviction, with authority, with freshness, and humor, and moral outrage. They startled me awake from my middle-class point of view. They sang eloquently about the most important things—love, class, race, history, poverty, family, death, joy—in a voice deeply elegant, and comprehensible, and musically powerful. They were written with terrific energy, containment, exuberance, emotion, wit, and shapeliness, and they had the authenticity of something made under the pressure and inspiration of a sense of great necessity. They had his distinctive, clear, sweet-moving, furious intimacy, a sense of actual people's lives. The well-madeness of the poems reminded me of George Herbert, and their inclusiveness and heart of Whitman. (Years later, after I'd introduced Phil at a reading at New York University, I asked him whether the introduction was all right, and he laughed and said, "The links with Shakespeare and Keats—what's not to like?!")

When I first was reading him, I wrote him a fan letter. I said something like, you have rescued lives not written of before, you are a hero. And Phil wrote back, saying, I'm no hero, I'm just someone who refuses to forget some men and women who were heroes. And he said, are you a writer? Your letter makes me think you are. Good luck with your writing!

So I propped some books of his on a shelf over my desk, where I could see them every day and be reminded of the integrity and music and courage possible in poetry. (But is it courage, if you're not afraid? In poems and in person, Phil has seemed to me to have, instead of fear, alertness, confidence, realism, wit, and a disdain for bullshit.)

In those days, I would walk around the apartment, sometimes, during my kids' naps. I'd go for long walks through the rooms, down the hall and back, holding one of my favorite books to my heart—often Phil's—hoping osmosis might teach me how to do whatever it was he did with egotism, with the speaker's self, so that the people and things in his poems shone through—the light being on them, rather than on himself.

(And now that I'm thinking about my early reading of his factory poems, his Detroit poems, his war poems, I'm realizing that his singing of lives not previously seen by a lot of people as worthy of song was one of the sources [along with Adrienne Rich, Muriel Rukeyser, Gwendolyn Brooks, and Ruth Stone] that prepared me to be more ready to see my [woman's] life as worthy of song.)

It's exhilarating to think of the depth and breadth of Phil's gifts to the generations of poets since those early days. Our landscape is radically richer because of him. Book after book, he has nourished and informed us. When I heard he'd been named our new poet laureate, I laughed out loud and pumped my fist in the air!

And he's such a lively and forthright critic; over the years, he has given me essential help with my poems. His eye for sentimentality, for the wrong word, for cliché, for idealization, has been impeccable. One of his critiques that has been of the broadest benefit to me had to do with line "breaks"—how we end one line and begin the next. I had finally figured out why I was leaving the small words—the articles and prepositions—at the ends of the lines, wanting to begin lines with nouns: I wanted my lines to look nothing like the end-stopped, rhymed hymn-lines of my childhood, which were my craft's secret model. (Secret from me until I was about fifty!) And Phil said, "Well, Sharon," in that crackly melodic mischievous voice, "not all of us went to your church when we were growing up! So, for us, why not do the first quatrain according to that tradition, to establish that norm, and *then* start to do the variations on it?!" That helped me with every poem since. And his pointing out, teasing and affectionate, my insular point of view, made it possible for me to get beyond myself sometimes.

When I think of Philip Levine's poems, what I think of first is the pleasure their beauty and power and down-home quality of reliable, mysterious, surprising truth has given us. And I think of the power of the poems' anger—the profound function, for a society, which its art can have. It is so important to know who we're mad at and why, and to sing it! Phil is making, with his flexible, ardent line, with his wise eye and impeccable ear, and with the rage and love of his heart, book after book of beautiful powerful near-living near-creatures—these voices of our histories, and of our nation's and species' crimes and hopes and heroisms, these poems we live and swear by.

So Enough

JANUARY GILL O'NEIL

In 1996, I was about to start my second year of study in the graduate Creative Writing Program at New York University. Sharon Olds and Galway Kinnell were my professors, and when I told Galway I wanted to work with Phil Levine as my thesis advisor, he looked at me with the straightest face possible and said, "Well, he's not as *crass* as he used to be."

Crass? Really? My first thought was, "I thought you two were friends." Once I picked my jaw up off the floor, I wondered whether I was about to make the biggest mistake of my life. Was my skin thick enough to stand up to Phil's legendary critiques? Would he make me cry?

Known primarily as a working-class poet, Phil shows a range of human emotions and failings in his poetry as he holds everything up against the complexities of everyday life. He's considered a poet's poet, writing much in his early- to mid-career about life in Detroit. He is a craftsman in the artless art of making the ordinary extraordinary. He's also known to keep a student's feet to the fire. If you make a bold statement in your poetry, in Phil's classes you needed to have the chops to back it up.

For me, Phil was the first poet I had read who made the working life poetic. He made the grease under one's fingernails poetic. He made Detroit everyone's hometown. Who knew universal joints could be poetic? His gritty style gave a certain dignity to factory life. And his mastery of poetic forms is an aspect of his work often overlooked. Two of my favorite books by Phil are *What Work Is* and his Pulitzer Prize–winning collection *The Simple Truth*.

Phil's straightforwardness in addressing the reader has always endeared me to his poetry. If poetry has a "fourth wall," as in stage acting where the dialogue is spoken directly to the audience, then Phil attempts to hook the reader in and truly bring him or her into the poem, something I've always strived to do in my work.

Well, Phil did not make me cry. He did what any dedicated teacher does: he made me better. Although Phil was a tough critic, he was generous with his time and his words. He cared enough to tell me whether I was going in the right direction or simply writing a piece of junk. And he did that more than once. It was important for me to work with someone whose strengths were in areas I thought were my weakest. He also urged me to read more outside of class so I could become the poet who would be ready to write a good poem at a moment's notice.

Studying with a talented writer is a real gift, no matter how famous or how many books he or she has published. Phil was more than a mentor. He was a physical representation of how I wanted to live in the world as a practicing poet. He gave his time to us, encouraged us to experience life in the real world, and pushed us to question everything. I knew that to be the kind of poet I wanted to be, a part of me had to change to practice this vocation. In other words, Phil taught me it was okay to make an ass out of myself. Through the weekly routine of wringing every last ounce of experience out of my poems, Phil taught me persistence. He told me that if I stuck with writing poetry—because so many creative writing students go in other directions after graduation—I'd probably write a few hundred poems during my poetic lifetime. But I should look for the occasion to push myself into an uncomfortable space to do my best work—I would need to make myself available to the process when those occasions occur.

Thirteen years later, I was able to write to him and share some good news: my first book, *Underlife*, was being published by CavanKerry Press. Finding a publisher can be a soul-crushing experience. But here I was, about to publish my very first collection. And Phil was right—the further away in years I was from grad school, the less confidence I had in my abilities. Sure, I could write, even publish a book. But during those years away from NYU without the safety net of having a regular routine, making a space for poetry, I felt lost. It really wasn't until I connected with virtual writing groups that bloomed all over the Internet in the late 2000s that I found the courage to write and share poems again. Now I understand that writing a good poem is about more than craft or technical proficiency or blind love of the word. It is this, and it is more. I wanted Phil to know what I had come to know.

In late 2009, I mailed a letter to Phil with a copy of *Underlife*. When the package dropped over the mailbox door, I felt this huge sense of relief. Closure, maybe. At the risk of being crass, to use Galway's word, I'll share excerpts of Phil's response to me. Some moments are worth sharing, and receiving this letter was certainly one of those moments.

January 22, 2010

Dear January,

Thanks so much for sending the new collection. I do remember several poems from either the class or your thesis . . . It was wonderful to discover what you've been up to since you left NYU; I knew you'd become a mother, but I hadn't known that that fact and the child had worked their way into your poetry. I truly believe that becoming a parent adds something to what we write; until that moment we can allow ourselves to be our own children, but the fact of that child ends all that. For a mother I'm sure it's more powerful than for a father; I take that back—I'm not sure at all. Both roles are mysterious.

. . . You know, I've finally retired, but I had so many marvelous classes, so many wonderful young poets. What a lucky man I was. People ask me if I miss it, & of course I do . . . I just thought it was time to go . . . And I just turned 82, so enough.

So much for eighty-two! Being chosen United States Poet Laureate is a well-deserved honor for a man who has devoted himself to perfecting his craft. I've known Phil to be the consummate writer who takes pleasure in the process of creation, ultimately creating a new way of seeing an object, or an event, or even a person. And if you don't think so, "then you haven't heard a word."

Finding Levine

GREG PAPE

I started classes at Fresno State in the fall of 1964. I had the vague idea that
I would study law. My first class as a pre-law English major, Business Law
101, met at 8 a.m. in a large, crowded auditorium. The instructor lectured
with a microphone, and the sound of his voice hissing and popping through
the faulty sound system had the almost immediate effect of inducing sleep.
Later in the day, after lunch and coffee, I went to my Introduction to Litera-
ture class taught by the poet Peter Everwine. Peter was a soft-spoken man
with a Fu-Manchu mustache, a smile like the Buddha, and when he read a
poem the words seemed to hover in the air and give off light. He must have
noticed my enthusiasm for poetry and at some point recommended I take a
class from Philip Levine. So I went looking for Levine. I asked around, and I
heard things: "he's brilliant," "he's hilarious," "he's intimidating," "he lives
and breathes poetry." Of course, I hadn't read a thing he had written, but on
campus at that time his presence was in the air.

In high school I was in an English class taught by Mario Chavez, who had
mentioned Levine in passing as we were reading the poetry of John Keats.
Chavez had taken at least one class from Levine, and Keats's poetry, Chavez
intimated, was a gift Levine had given him. And Chavez passed that gift along

to me. Keats's poems cast a spell so that reading his lines was like hearing my own secret thoughts take shape:

> O Solitude! If I must with thee dwell,
>> Let it not be among the jumbled heap
>> Of murky buildings; climb with me the steep,—
> Nature's observatory—whence the dell,
> Its flowery shapes, its river's crystal swell, . . .

With Keats in my backpack I'd hop on my Yamaha and head for the San Joaquin River or the foothills of the Sierras and commune with those "Great Spirits . . . standing apart"

> Upon the forehead of the age to come;
> These, these will give the world another heart,
> And other pulses. Hear ye not the hum
> Of mighty workings? . . .
> Listen awhile, ye nations, and be dumb.

Back on campus I continued my search for Levine. I went to his office, but he wasn't there. Browsing the bookstore, I found a fresh stack of paperbacks with his name on the front cover and his picture on the back. He looked more like an athlete than a professor, which made him seem approachable. He was standing in the sunshine at the edge of what looked like the San Francisco Bay, a smile on his face, a book in his clasped hands. I opened the book at random and read "An Abandoned Factory, Detroit." It sounded nothing like Keats, but it cast a spell. "The gates are chained, the barb-wire fencing stands, / An iron authority against the snow . . ." Standing in the aisle of the bookstore I was transported to a place where "the hum of mighty workings" was stopped, "caught / In the sure margin of eternity." And the abandoned factory was a monument to "the loss of human power . . . the loss of years, the gradual decay of dignity." It was a chilling experience to read that poem. How did he do that, I wondered? How did he put me outside the chained gate and get me to imagine the lives of the people who worked there "hour by hour," year by year until they were gone? As I read, the words turned into the scene and the feelings, and I seemed to bring in details and images of my own only suggested by the poem. Levine wrote "broken windows," and I saw the jagged edges of the glass, the shards on the concrete floor. I could hear and feel the rhythm and the rhymes, but I wasn't aware of the pattern. I didn't know there was such a thing as meter. I had been making up poems and songs and stories since I was a child, but it wasn't until my junior year in high school after the Cuban Missile Crisis and the assassination of President John F. Kennedy (the announcement came over the intercom as we were reading Keats in Mario Chavez's class) that I decided to seriously write poems. When I read Levine, I thought just maybe I could learn to make a poem that would hold together. Hold what together? I wasn't sure. Me? The world?

When I finally tracked him down, he was just leaving his office, dressed in white shorts, heading for the tennis courts. I may have introduced myself. I may have asked him if I could take his poetry class. What I clearly remember is handing him my most recent poem and standing there while he glanced over it, watching as a vaguely pained expression came over his face. He handed the poem back and said, "Come back during office hours, and bring something better than this," and he walked off. I stood there and read the poem again to myself and thought, "Yeah, I see what you mean." Levine didn't know it yet, but I had found my mentor. That night I read and reread *On the Edge*. High on the power of the poems, I wrote something better than what I had first handed to Levine. A couple of days later I stopped by his office. He was busy with another student, so I placed the poem on his desk and left. I would come back another day and ask him whether I could take his poetry class.

Around this same time I picked up a copy of *Howl* for seventy-five cents. I was blown away by the fierce, incantatory power of its long looping lines. I remember reading the whole first section aloud to my friend and roommate Terry Holmes, who stared at me dumbfounded and finally said something like, "Far out, man! You know," he said, "Ginsberg is coming to campus on Friday. We should go see him."

That Friday we sat on the grass at the amphitheater at Fresno State with hundreds of others and listened to Ginsberg chant his poems as he accompanied himself on the harmonium. Just as the performance was ending, I saw Levine walking toward us. "Hey, Pape," he said, and squatted down beside me. He had my poem in his hand. He pointed to some lines in the middle, "Here's where the poem starts. The rest is shit." I may be misremembering. He probably said something funnier, such as, "The first ten lines sound like Little Lord Fauntleroy imitating Ferlinghetti." Still, the message was the same. He was telling me what I needed to hear. And then he said, "Why don't you come sit in on my class next week." He handed me the poem with his markings on it, slapped me on the shoulder and walked off. That was my first workshop with Levine. I was deeply pleased and honored that he had read the poem, carried it around, and singled me out of that crowd to give my poem and me a clear and honest response.

Over the next few years I would take every class I could from Levine. All that I had heard was true; he was brilliant, hilarious, utterly honest, constantly challenging us to dig deeper, to write like our lives depended on it, which they did. I felt lucky to be accepted into those classes and to be a part of a community of young poets including Larry Levis, David St. John, Roberta Spear, Ernesto Trejo, and others, galvanized by Levine's energy, humanity, and fierce commitment to the art of poetry.

I learned so much in those years from Levine and my classmates and my other terrific teachers at Fresno State: Peter Everwine, Robert Mezey, and Charles Hanzlicek. We read everything from the Bible to the Beats. When we read Frost and Yeats and Auden, we learned to scan and write in various meters as a way of paying attention to what was going on in the poems. We learned to listen to and to hear what we read and what we wrote. If poetry was a kind of guarded secret in high school, at Fresno State it was a live and relevant public art. We read aloud to each other in the classroom and at Cafe Midi, and later at gatherings of resistance to the Vietnam War.

When Levine returned from a year in Spain, he brought Spanish, Latin American, and world poetry back with him. His classes were animated with readings of Miguel Hernández, Claudio Rodriguez, Gloria Fuertes, and many other poets whom very few Americans had ever heard of before. Just as he had given Mario Chavez the gift of Keats, he was giving us Lorca, Neruda, Vallejo, Milosz, Herbert, Holub, Hikmet, Montale, and Pavese. I still have many battered paperbacks and mimeographed sheets of poetry in translation from that time. But much of the work of translation was yet to be done.

One of the last classes I took from Levine was a translation workshop cotaught with Jose Elgorriaga. Half the class was made up of Spanish majors, the other half poets. Elgorriaga and Levine alternated between clowning around, weighing and debating the best way to render some Spanish phrase into an approximate equivalent in English, and giving passionate readings of poems in Spanish and English. The class was a joy and seemed to consume the semester. It was a great lesson in imagination and craft to try to inhabit those poems in another language and bring them, still living, into English. I lugged my hardbound Velasquez Spanish Dictionary everywhere I went, and I spent many wonderful hours going over poems with Ernesto Trejo, my Mexican classmate who was perfectly bilingual.

It felt then like we were a part of some sort of renaissance in which poets from all over the world were working shoulder to shoulder making poems out of the chaos of a world constantly at war and a culture that seemed to deny every truth that tried to surface, a culture that sang the loud praises of democracy as it beat down any voice of dissent.

Levine let us know that the work of a poet was hard and worthy work, that it was the work itself and how that work spoke from an individual to a shared humanity that mattered. His gift to us as a teacher and as a poet is a lasting one. His poems are about people whose lives are tough, people who struggle to hold on to their dignity and their sanity, people who work to keep their souls alive. He writes about soldiers, prisoners, factory workers, teachers, laborers of all kinds, men and women and children who experience hardship, failure, exploitation, oppression, and, because they are alive, they also experience joy and occasionally triumph.

As a young man I loved Levine's audacity, his sense of humor, his eloquent anger, his generous spirit. I still do. I'd like to say of Levine what Levine said of Keats: "He remains a wellspring to which all of us might go to refresh our belief in the value of this art."

On the Meeting of García Lorca

KATHLEEN PEIRCE

It's the late eighties. I'm with Gerald Stern and Phil Levine in the kitchen of
the house Phil's renting for a semester as a visiting professor at Iowa, where
I've either graduated or I'm still enrolled. It's a painter's house, somebody I
haven't met who's gone somewhere else to think and work. The house is full
of things I could spend the day looking at, and the three of us fill it further.
Perspective feels strange because nothing there belongs to any of us, and close
because it's a home, though no part of this is ordinary. I think I remember
a dark bed built into a wooden alcove off the living room, three walls to hold
sleep in, a near surround. I wanted that. I still do. There were paintings with
a lot of black. There may have been, I'm almost sure, vigorous plants grow-
ing in and out of the kitchen window, but who would have such a window
in town? There was coffee, surely, and one or two of us eating something
while leaning over the kitchen sink. Jerry and Phil are talking, talking, going
over everything, biting at each other and laughing together in the same sen-
tences. We might have just come back from a drive in the country, possibly
from looking for quilts the rural women on the outskirts of Iowa City cut and
sewed their worn clothes to make and maybe were willing to sell. We had
begun to hang quilts in our living rooms in those days. Probably we pulled
over for tomatoes or peaches or corn. Years will pass before any of my poems

will mean anything to anybody but me. Jerry hasn't yet collapsed with heart trouble, Phil hasn't yet called to give me the news. I'm five years into a marriage I'm sure will last forever. Jerry's in love, or about to be. Phil has Franny. We're healthy. Poetry's hard. I am in love with my life. Phil understands that my hometown is a factory town. He's the first person who's asked me to say more about candling eggs in the basement of the Sara Lee plant in Moline. I laugh telling him about having to shout *push my eggs down, please* to the men who loaded the conveyor with the crates. I tell him I believe I thought about sex nonstop through every shift that winter. He asks me what my father did for a living. He understands that I think I've survived my childhood. I understand that he and Jerry have everything I think I want. Because I adore them I believe they are always adored. I am so strangely at home with them I think they always were at home in their lives. Phil says he has something for me, and leaves the room to get it. Could I be happier? Poetry is hard, and Phil has a beautiful gift for me. He comes back to the kitchen, Jerry's singing something, Phil passes me Lorca's *Poet in New York*. I'm about to enter my real life. He says the anger in it was a big help to him, and he hopes it will help me. He thinks it will. It did. It does.

Jabs, Uppercuts, and Kindness
The Humanity of Philip Levine

SAM PEREIRA

People fall into various categories when they think about and discuss moments of epiphany. There are those who create a daily documentation of these moments, and it almost always involves God in some way, shape, or form. There are those lacking such moments, and these are generally far too busy trying to stay afloat and alive to deal with such audacious considerations. Finally, there are the few who, because of some luck of the draw, find those magical moments in the form of another human being. For me, it occurred sometime around 1968, when God, or those unwitting administrative types at Fresno State, placed Phil Levine in front of budding new university students, including this stupid, small-town yokel.

Up until the late sixties, I had been relegated to living in a forgettable place in the San Joaquin Valley, a small community called Los Banos. We had cows. We had cow shit. We had churches. We had often recurring community mass get-togethers, usually connected to some church organization and referred to as "feeds." These gave the feeling that everything was about satisfying physical needs . . . chowing down for Jeezuz. So, when I left at eighteen for Fresno and what I was pretty sure would become a career of teaching English, I had no idea what was about to happen. Instinctively, I knew my plate was about to become a good deal more complex than it ever had been.

These were extraordinary times for everyone, but for someone living in virtual isolation, they were the illegal drugs I had been waiting for. Phil was an icon even then. His books—all two of them—were on bookshelves throughout Fresno. *Not This Pig* became a reference point more often than not, and it remains so today, several decades later. I knew that teaching was going to be the vehicle I needed to rely on for things like maintaining a roof over my head in old age, but I also knew that poetry was locked into place now and had replaced the usual small-town expectations I had known growing up.

Phil's classes were filled with people who would go on to become today's generation of established and respected poets. Sitting next to me for each workshop session, every class relating to form, each utterance from a man who was about to become synonymous with poetry in America, were writers like Larry Levis, David St. John, Greg Pape, Roberta Spear, Bruce Boston, Lance Patigian, and Michael Clifton. We felt anointed with power and we all believed we were on the verge of saying something worth hearing, worth reading. Much of what Phil gave us was the surprising realization that we were not even *close* to reaching this pinnacle. This is what happened: we worked, we said stupid things, we said reasonably smart things, and we became friends. Oh, and we were in awe of this man from Detroit, who for some reason known only to him, had decided to share his spirit for poetry with those of us willing to listen.

Education, as is so often the case with writing, didn't always come with the infusion of poetic devices. Sometimes it came in the form of just how to be an honorable and enlightened person in a world full of approaching pitfalls. Remember, it *was* the sixties! On one occasion, I recall being in a class on Twentieth-Century American Poetry—and weren't they all?—when a student who was better known for his luck at the track than for his writing blurted something disrespectful at a nun who happened to be taking the class. She had not said anything; was merely taking notes, as Phil talked. In spite of the antireligious nature many of us seemed to espouse during those times—young rebels that we insisted on being—the rest of the class knew she had done nothing to cause this outburst. Phil, outspoken poet and self-proclaimed anarchist, didn't laugh and didn't take sides with this loudmouth student. Instead, he asked the guy to leave his classroom. If there was ever any doubt in my mind up until then—and there was not—about the genuine humanity of Levine, it took a long, one-way trip to the moon on that day.

There was also a time soon after Fresno State that dealt with Iowa City, where Phil insisted I apply in 1972, because, he said, "You're applying to all these other places! Why would you *not* apply to Iowa?" I couldn't give him a good reason, and have always been grateful for that vote of confidence.

Once the MFA years ended, I came back to what one can only call madness. I took a job in management in the agricultural industry, so prevalent in California's San Joaquin Valley. For twenty-one years, I did the work asked; trying to write during the hours I had left over, which were never plentiful. During this time, through handwritten correspondences and visits to Fresno to just sit and talk and listen—mostly listen—to Phil and his lovely wife, Franny, I was allowed to hang on to the poetry, in spite of the world continually trying to kick it out of me.

There were a number of Saturdays when I would drive to Fresno and just show up on Phil's front doorstep, be invited in, have a glass of tea, and watch Saturday afternoon boxing on CBS. Another thing in common. The intricacies of boxing; its brutality and beauty. It was wonderful.

During one of these visits Phil decided to take my new car—a Dodge Challenger—out for a spin. I was honored! The guy from Detroit shifting gears down Van Ness Boulevard with me in the passenger seat, on the way to Old Doc's Liquors, where Phil would buy a nice bottle of red from what was probably an obscure Spanish vintner, while watching me load up my shopping cart with various gins, scotches, and vodkas. He knew, but would never condescend. In hindsight, he must have been imagining what I was doing to my body. I stopped. I survived. Not without homage due to Phil for putting up with a lot of bad judgments from me along the way.

One thing needs to be said outright here. Phil Levine did not and does not have patience for those who would choose to take an easy ride on the stallion Poetry. It takes a long time to get the attention of this great man, but once you are seen as real in Phil's eyes, there is little he would not do to help in what is universally understood to be a skill most people would find of use only to academics and the effete. When someone's love is real for poetry, Phil picks it up on his radar and beams it back at that person. The intensity is brutally magnificent and something any right-thinking writer should relish.

Over the years, I have come to depend on honest readings from Phil of work I have shown him. Mind you, one does not want to take advantage of these kindnesses—and they are kindnesses—but one should also never expect sugarcoating from Phil. If he likes something, he almost always offers up alternative ways of saying whatever you think you have so brilliantly put down; if he likes the last poem you showed him, this in no way indicates that he will like the one you place in front of him next. In fact, he has *hated* some of my work at times, to which I say now, with great feeling and from the bottom of my heart: *Thank you!*

Permission to Be

Philip Levine at Columbia, 1978

JEFFREY SKINNER

On the first day of our workshop Phil asked, "Are there any geniuses in this room?" No one raised a hand or said a word. "Good," Phil said. "I have nothing to teach a genius, and a genius doesn't need this class. Also, I am not a genius. If I were I wouldn't be teaching. I'd be writing genius poems. Now that *that's* out of the way, we can get to work."

This was a time when students were writing poems that sounded slick and smart but did not hold up under clear-eyed, bullshit-detecting scrutiny, which Phil was happy to provide. Other students wrote versions of the then-current mode—sincere, lyric-narrative poems that reliably contained, like the prize in a box of Cracker Jacks, an epiphany.

Tess Gallagher was all the rage, and in the middle of another workshop day Phil was obviously exasperated by the prospect of discussing yet another Gallagher knock-off. He suddenly struck the table with his knuckles, a light knock, and pushed the poem away toward the center of the conference table. He closed his eyes, and then just sat there, doing nothing. The author of the abandoned poem stared at Phil, her expression an anxious mix of terror, and hope beyond hope. The rest of us held our collective breath, not knowing what the hell to expect.

"Tess is *fine*," Phil said finally, "but if you're gonna steal, go back and steal from the old guys—go to Keats, go to Hardy. Find out why they're still around. See what you can do with that."

"Listen," he said, and took Hardy's "Transformations" from his notebook, and read it to us. Twice. Here's the poem:

Portion of this yew
Is a man my grandsire knew,
Bosomed here at its foot:
This branch may be his wife,
A ruddy human life
Now turned to a green shoot.

These grasses must be made
Of her who often prayed,
Last century, for repose;
And the fair girl long ago
Whom I often tried to know
May be entering this rose.

So, they are not underground,
But as nerves and veins abound
In the growths of upper air,
And they feel the sun and rain,
And the energy again
That made them what they were!

He let that sink in. In the silence, Phil was teaching. Then he picked up the poor woman's workshop poem and launched into the devastation.

Phil was my hero, my favorite poet. At Columbia I waited through three semesters of workshops for his arrival. He would love and praise my work. He would direct my thesis. We would become friends. This was the plan.

And in fact the time for workshop with Phil did arrive, though it had seemed extraordinarily long in coming, as long as a kid's Christmas Eve, or any distant event the imagination has magnified by desire.

The first few classes I spent in silent awe. We had been expecting a poetry god, and Phil did not disappoint: he was larger than life, tough and wiry like his poems, with a blithe confidence in his powers—he could, for example, see right through poems with his x-ray vision. He was unapologetically masculine and moved and carried himself with subdued grace, as if he were still capable of hard manual labor. His humor was of a type I instantly recognized from my Long Island upbringing—caustic, and deflating of the least hint of pretension. Though he claimed to be from Detroit, he easily could have fit in with the working-class New York men that had surrounded me throughout boyhood. Except, *this* was a man who also wrote sublime poetry.

Then one class it happened. Phil shuffled through the pile of poems in front of him and pulled out *my very own poem*! But instead of asking me to read it, and then soliciting student responses—which was the convention—he read my poem out loud himself, in his nasal voice, accompanied by a barely discernable, finely honed edge of sarcasm. At least, that's what I heard. Probably just my nerves, I thought to myself. I hoped no one else had noticed.

Phil finished reading and paused briefly. I looked furtively around the table. And then without ceremony he proceeded to eviscerate my poem. He tore it a new one. He called it a "B movie" poem. Sometimes we were in the mood for a B movie, he granted, and B movies could be entertaining in their way. In a trivial way. Then he talked about some of his favorite B movies, most from the thirties and forties. He ridiculed them, but also paid them homage, at least for taking people's minds off darker matters.

But that was the problem. Poems should contain those darker matters that B movies skirted. Sure, such faux art did satisfy some of our baser fantasies and desires. That didn't change the fact that they were . . . crap. Like my poem. My poem was crap.

Any comments?

There were none. I think we must have discussed the other workshop poems after that, but I have no recollection. I was in a blackout. The next thing I remember is walking out of the classroom and several of my fellow student poets gently patting my back and saying things like, "Don't worry, man—I hear he does that in every workshop," and "Oh, Jeff, are you are all right?"

I hurried from the building and went directly to the West End Cafe. I drank a beer and three shots of Seagram's Seven as quickly as I could, then left before any of my classmates arrived for the traditional postworkshop cocktail hour debriefing. I could not bear to suffer any further consolation.

What rose in me during the days and weeks after this class was not resignation or despair, but *anger*, anger and defiance. *No way this is the end of it, Levine,* I said to the looming figure in my mind. *I'm going to write other poems—much better poems—and you are going to like them, you are going to like my poems and you are going to like me. Yes, and you will direct my thesis, too!* I had many imaginary conversations with the poet-god Philip Levine, who had destroyed me. I could not wait to prove him wrong. I seethed, and I wrote.

My reaction could have been otherwise. I had seen students whose confidence was destroyed by workshop comments. A few had simply dropped out. I was once talking with another student in the hall when a woman burst from Phil's office, sobbing. I found out later that Phil had turned down her thesis; it *wasn't good enough*, he had told her. She would not get a degree.

Others continued after taking critical beatings, but made inner adjustments. Their comments in workshop afterward became reflexively qualified, their general manner a kind of meek hesitation. Their expectations as to what the rest of their time in the program might give them, and what they themselves might add to poetry, were diminished.

Teachers have power.

I don't know why I didn't react this way. I have come to believe that in addition to talent, a kind of stubbornness is necessary for life as a poet. Or maybe it is defiance.

Whatever one calls it, the result is a refusal to believe when some part of the world tells you that what you've made is no damn good, implying that you should *not quit your day job*. The desire to redouble your effort when faced with rejection is essential. This desire rose up in me without summons—and I used it to good purpose with Phil, though that was hardly the last time in my life I've made use of it. *Ars longa, vita breva* . . . for the artist, the power to reject rejection is the gift that keeps giving.

I think Phil recognized my reaction and respected it. He knew that his way of teaching made use of strong challenge, and he had seen students react to it differently. He'd been teaching long enough to see what worked, who survived and who didn't. In any case I *did* begin to write better poems that semester, and Phil began to say good things about them. I asked him to direct my thesis. Before he agreed, he asked how old I was. When I told him— twenty-eight—he nodded and said, approvingly: "You're not a kid; you're a grown-up man. Good."

During our meetings about the thesis I remember very little discussion of the actual poems—"These you should take out; the others are fine," was the extent of Phil's counsel in that arena. We talked mostly about my life—my job, my wife, where I'd come from, what my parents were like, sports I played, books I read, movies I loved. Phil would ask questions about these things as if he really was interested, and then respond with moments from his life. We connected. We liked each other.

"You're a grown-up man." I see now that he meant this as both compliment and challenge. He made many other simple but affirming comments every time I saw him, at Columbia, and in all our encounters over the years since. He wrote me countless references for jobs, grants, etc. When I started a literary press with my wife, Phil judged our first poetry contest, and the book remains one of our best sellers. He advised me when I was disconsolate about my place in the art, and he celebrated when good things came to me. We weren't frequently in touch, but I relied on his presence in the world for continuing inspiration.

Once, when I hadn't seen or talked to Phil in several years, I had a very serious motorcycle accident. I lay in the hospital, not at all sure I'd survive, and he called, having heard about the accident through the poetry grapevine. We talked for a long time. He told a story of his brief experience with motorcycles. He made me laugh, and he called me *honey*—this rough guy from Detroit. A few weeks later, another call.

I don't know the right words to say how much Phil Levine has meant to me, as poet, as man, as model. No—in terms of my life as a poet, there is one word: everything.

When I first encountered Phil, so many years ago, I made a study of his way of being in the world—his combination of rigor and gruff humor, his surprising sweetness, how he did not suffer fools—and I saw a way through my own life. It wasn't that I wanted to *be* Phil. The lesson of Phil's example said to me, simply, that I could be what I was. And that had to be enough, really—any other way was bullshit. For whatever it's worth, that's what I've done.

To See What It Was Worth

TOM SLEIGH

When I first met Phil Levine almost thirty years ago, the sun coming into the window was the weak pale sun of spring in Boston. We were sitting in a parlor room that looked vaguely Victorian, vaguely Yankee. Phil was teaching at Tufts University one semester a year, and this was the house that the university had given him: the furniture was quasi-antique, the chairs were the overstuffed kind that swallow you up but still manage to feel uncomfortable, as if to rebuke you for expecting comfort in the first place. It was the sort of house that had tall, narrow windows, tea trays, and etchings of New England landscapes or scenes of colonial history on the walls.

Phil mocked, in a genial way, the house's faux-historic pretensions, partly as a way of putting me at ease, but also trying to find out what kind of sense of humor I had. It was also his characteristically generous way of offering younger people immediate terms of equality: he didn't stand on ceremony, seemed to suffer not at all from "Great Man Syndrome," and neither expected, nor brooked, obeisance from younger writers. That was immediately relieving, but also a little daunting: here was a man who had his wits about him, who missed nothing, who took in what you said and how you said it, so that he could weigh it, test it, and see how it sat with his own taste. That quality of alertness, of giving yourself over momentarily to another person's viewpoint in order to see what it was worth, is one of the first things that I learned from Phil. He was taking my measure, assessing my taste by testing it, as Keats once said, on his own pulses.

We were on the subject of Philip Larkin when Phil asked me whether I knew Larkin's poem "At Grass," about racehorses put out to pasture. I'd read it, but no, I couldn't say I "knew" it. As we talked, he quoted parts of it from memory, and lingered over the line "Till wind distresses tail and mane." He loved Larkin's use of the word *distresses* for the way the wind blew the tail and mane about, but also for the double entendre of the tresses coming undone. And he told me that racehorses always have their tails and manes done up before the race, and so dis-tressing them, and having the wind do it, marked off the racehorse from the pure horse—the horse that kicks up its heels and runs away from the human world of jockeys, fame, and sweepstakes.

The more we talked, the more I felt the acuteness of his intelligence, how varied and eclectic his taste was, and that taste itself was a kind of ethical standard: it wasn't so much about what you liked and didn't like about a writer's language, though of course that was immensely important, but what the texture of the writer's mind felt like: that texture was historically specific and politically implicated, and at the same time, always a bit of a mirage. This recognition was what impressed me most—his own skepticism about his own fine distinctions. He knew that fine distinctions and sensibility run the risk of being merely eccentric, merely personal. But I also remember him saying how bored he was with all the talk denouncing "the solipsism" of young writers: what else did a young writer have except for solipsism?

As we traded back and forth favorite Larkin lines, at a certain point he changed tack by saying what a conservative old shit Larkin was in his taste for music and literature. That kind of clear-eyed skepticism was also instructive, but even more so was the way Phil said it—humorously, stepping around the role that Yvor Winters, Phil's old teacher, liked to play: the literary moralist, the defender of the mind against the irrational and unreason. Over the years, how many times have I seen Phil roll his eyes at the various village explainers of the poetry world: best to keep a healthy distance from any kind of orthodoxy. Phil also brought up Larkin's limitations as a literary critic and Thatcherite. Larkin's dislike of modernist writers struck Phil as cant: Larkin acting out a role that he relished more for the figure he cut than for the judgments advanced: you had to be wary of your own vanity, of adopting some role for effect.

Phil's humor also demonstrated the corollary lesson of what you might call one-downmanship, as opposed to one-upmanship: far preferable to joke at your own pretensions to authority than end up wearing those views like a uniform. Phil has always been allergic to dogmatic pronouncements, no matter who issues them. Traditional, avant-garde, it's like listening to hard-line Stalinists argue over ideological purity. But Phil's love of particular poems and poets has always kept him open to chance and change.

What T. S. Eliot wrote of Henry James—that he had "a mind so fine no idea can violate it"—seems even more true of Phil: the elegance and complexity of Phil's mind has never been seduced by its own capacities. Unlike James, Phil has resisted the temptation to mistake his own thoughts and feelings for Consciousness. And as great a writer as James is, his self-consciousness—once likened to watching a rhinoceros push a pea from one end of his cage to another—has never infected Phil's understanding of his own role as a poet. He's always been wary of his own, and other people's, impulses to make him fit some poetic mold or other. If I've learned anything from Phil, it's this: that nobody really knows the kind of poet they are . . . and that nobody is a poet, except at the moment when they're actually writing a poem.

Philip Levine and the
Hands of Time

DAVID ST. JOHN

Among those poets who have been Philip Levine's students at some point in their lives—and I am assuming that includes almost all of the poets in this collection—there is a clear consensus that there simply was not and is not any more passionate, wise, hilarious, useful, fearsome, brilliant, loyal, or inspiring teacher of poetry, as literature and craft, than Philip Levine.

As I've told many times, I was eighteen years old and a freshman at Fresno State College when Larry Levis introduced me to Philip Levine. Over the se-mester break between Fall and Spring, Larry—who'd seen a few of my early inept poems—came up to me at a rock concert we both happened to be at and told me that Phil was teaching a beginning poetry writing class that next semester. It was something he didn't always do, and Larry said that I had to take Levine's class. Larry was rarely insistent about anything, so I immediately said, Of course. Larry later made sure that I met Phil, and with both Larry and Phil as my models, my life in poetry had begun.

It would be impossible to overstate Levine's charisma at that moment in the spring of 1968. Phil looked like a cross between Woody Guthrie and Paul Newman in *Hud*—lean, muscular, intense. For someone of such an urban background, Levine seemed incredibly connected to the earth, the land. Phil had—and still has—an extraordinary sense of humor, and I've always loved watching some recognition of an absurdity crackle in his eyes just before the delivery of the exact, withering comment it would deserve. He was capable of being fall-down funny and vulgar as well as capable of talking with exquisite complexity about John Donne (or Robert Herrick or Philip Larkin or Emily Dickinson) in a way that was at once practical and devotional.

Phil taught from an anthology that was historical, called *Poetry in English*, and his class was my real education in the tradition of poetry. We might be talking about one of the student poems in our beginning workshop, and Phil would find a phrase he admired (or pretended to admire) and he would say to us, "This reminds me of that moment in Emily Dickinson when . . ." or, "You know, in Whitman, when he . . ." and then he would read us these great passages as instruction and example.

This did something else as well. His method connected us (and our own pitiful poems) to the larger tradition of poetry. It made us believe that what we were writing was actually in conversation with the poems and poets who had come before us. It allowed us to understand that poems don't come out of a vacuum and to recognize the necessity of knowing the poetry of one's own language and poetic tradition. I think this may be one of the most important things I have ever learned.

Yet Levine's knowledge of poetry in translation, especially poetry from Spanish and Polish, also completely transformed my understanding of what poetry could do and be. In my later years as Phil's student at Fresno State, I began to understand that poetry existed not only in the context and conversation of the poetry of—and in—my own language, but in the context and traditions of poems from all around the world. This too felt like a stunning thing to discover, and the world of poetry opened up for me again.

Just a few years ago, for a profile she was writing on me for *Ploughshares*, the poet Susan Terris asked me to talk about first meeting Phil during those early years in Fresno. This is what I said:

Levine was the most charismatic adult I'd ever met—brilliant, wittier than anyone on the planet except Oscar Wilde, and just as vicious when he wanted to be, and a poet who was about to explode onto the landscape of American poetry. He introduced me to a Who's Who of American poetry: Adrienne Rich, Galway Kinnell, W. S. Merwin, Mark Strand, Charles Wright, Donald Justice—all poets who would become friends in later years, and Justice, of course, was my teacher at Iowa.

Fresno was a quiet town then, and poets came to read and see Levine, so it was great fun. It was also the sixties, and nuts in its own special way, of course.

One of the things all of Phil's students treasured were the extraordinarily detailed comments he would write on our poems. Always written in fountain pen, his precise line edits and more general comments in the margins served to focus our poems and to allow us to see our poems—and their possible revisions—in a completely new light. I have saved every one of those drafts with Phil's comments on them from the very first, knowing their importance to me. Even when he was living abroad in Spain (during the time when I was an undergraduate), and trying to escape his students, he would read and make line edits on the poems that I sent him with a care that was remarkable. He did this, of course, at the expense of his own time and writing, something that took me far too long to recognize and understand. Of course, Phil's own poems are models of poetic instruction in both their vision and their craft.

Perhaps now is the place to say that Phil was also a model to us all, a living model, of how to be a writer in the world—an example of how to be an engaged and consistently humane presence in a culture that undervalued both poetry and, it has often seemed, its own citizens as well. His presence was fiercely political in the most human way; that is, he reminded us that poetry creates empathy for those marginalized by their societies, and that to live responsibly and to write with conscience were crucial elements of being a poet. Phil taught us that skepticism and a sense of humor were essential to any life, but especially to a poet's life.

He also taught us that poetry is often about time—about how the use of memory in poetry helps us to recuperate the past, those events and individuals we have lost to time. Poetry is able to help us to recover and bring back into the present of the poem what otherwise might seem gone from a life forever. For Levine, the acts of memory and reflection were, in his poetry, constant threads in an ongoing poetic reckoning with his own experiences and the details of his own past, including his sketches of those men and women who helped to make up that past, and who were themselves now gone. But one of Levine's lessons about time was, for me, of a more profoundly immediate nature. There was nothing abstract about this lesson whatsoever, and it came from fiction, not from poetry at all.

One spring, I was taking a class from Phil on contemporary fiction that was being held in one of the auxiliary classroom buildings—like a series of trailers really—called San Ramon. They were adequate classrooms, if not terrifically substantial, and they were no worse than any other classroom. They were both new and temporary. We sat in the usual half-desks that torture students everywhere, and Phil sat at a small table at the front of the room, facing the students. Above him on the front wall was the round black-rimmed/white-faced industrial clock typical of most classrooms.

Our class was held just after lunch, and on this particular day I remember that I was late and so was hurrying across campus. I tried to come in quietly so as not to disturb the discussion; then I noticed that Phil himself hadn't yet arrived, which was unusual. I slid into a desk and waited along with the rest of the class.

That day we were discussing one of Phil's favorite recent books, one I had already read at his suggestion, Frank Conroy's remarkable memoir *Stop-Time*. We were all looking forward to the discussion, having discovered during the semester that Levine was as brilliant talking about fiction as he was discussing poetry. Another few minutes passed after I sat down and Phil came in. He walked to the front of the room and then sat at the small table. He looked at us in a way that seemed both bemused and puzzled, as if he were thinking, Where did *they* all come from?

We all had our copies of the book on our desks in front us, alongside our notebooks, ready to be responsible students of creative writing. Then Phil began to lecture. He hadn't taken out his own copy of *Stop-Time* and put it on the table in front of him, as he usually might. In fact, he clearly hadn't brought his own copy of the book with him at all. Still, he began to lecture about time, about the nature of time and memory, about how Conroy played with these elements throughout the course of his memoir, and how he so brilliantly manipulated us, his readers, in those manipulations of narrative time.

While speaking, Phil had gotten up from the table and had begun to walk back and forth behind the table as he talked; then he'd walk over to one of those grey metal media carts (they seemed to be in every classroom awaiting some mysterious use) that stood at the front and side of the room. He'd put his hand on the cart somewhat thoughtfully as he lectured, then he would walk back behind the table, still talking about time. Phil had now begun to talk about what time does to us, how time wants often to destroy us and take us with it. Basically, he said, time (Time) has only one message for us: it continues and we do not.

I had come to know Phil well enough during these years to realize that he was, well, not drunk exactly, but eloquently soused. He'd clearly had a great wine with his lunch. He was so calm and composed, however, that I don't think anyone else in the room had a clue about this. That is, until he pulled the chair away from the small table and moved it directly beneath the clock on the wall above him, the clock students stared at day in and day out in their academic imprisonment in that San Ramon classroom.

Phil stepped up on the chair, reached above him, and took the huge round clock in both of his hands. He gripped it so that his fingers slid slightly behind the black rim of the clock, then in one incredibly authoritative gesture, he pulled that clock right out of the wall and ripped it off of its wires. He stepped down off the chair and walked over to the grey steel media cart and deposited the clock on its top shelf, where the stopped clock stared up like an open eye at the classroom ceiling.

He never stopped speaking once. He continued to lecture fluidly and fluently throughout this whole spectacular event—he was lecturing about time, even as he defiantly stopped time in our ridiculous and completely artificial classroom. What I remember vividly was looking up to see that the hole in the wall in front of me—the place where the clock had been—was not, as I had expected it to be, round like the clock itself but, instead, square, so as to match and hold the square metal box of clockworks on the back of the clock. I have always considered this to be the day's second revelation.

For the entire remainder of that semester the torn, naked red-and-black wires that had once been attached to the clock dangled down from the empty square in the wall up above Phil's table. The clock itself also sat for the remainder of that semester on the top of the steel grey media cart. No one came to repair the clock. No one came to start time again in Phil's classroom. Either no one cared, or no one dared. After all, if the man who taught in that classroom could stop time, then who knew what else he might be able to do?

The Poems We Carry

BRIAN TURNER

Winter, 2004. Mosul.

As part of the 3rd Stryker Brigade Combat Team, I've deployed to Iraq and taken part in numerous missions for several months. I'm a sergeant and an infantryman. I'm also a poet. When the late-night raids conclude, the depositions are filled out, and the prisoners are turned over to the military police, who drink coffee and tell stupid jokes to one another to lessen the tedium of 3 a.m., my platoon heads back to our hooches to get some rack time. And me? Before laying my head down to sleep, I switch on a red-lens flashlight (so as not to bother other exhausted soldiers sleeping in mummy bags nearby) to jot down the day's events and thoughts while they're still relatively fresh in my mind, before they blur into all that tomorrow's missions might bring. I'm writing in a seventy-page, college-ruled notebook with a ballpoint pen. And I've been doing this for months, notebook by notebook.

These notebooks offer a space for passages of prose and line sketches drawn from a bird's-eye view; the pages fill with depictions of ambushes, vehicle and foot patrols, moments when bullets are stripped of their brassy jackets to carry the noise of gunpowder into the world. As the weeks pass by, a few fragments of poetry begin to appear. A couplet here. A stanza there. Whole poems emerge. In mid-to-late February, I cover my ears with headphones and listen to Queens of the Stone Age playing "No One Knows," over and over. Heavy rock, with an insistent rhythmic drive—the music creates an aural wall between the rest of the world and me. A buffer of sound that isn't war. It is in this moment that I write the poem "Here, Bullet." It takes a little less than fifteen minutes to write, and I quickly excise the three additional lines I've scrawled in the margin. I cross out the word *finish* and write in the word *complete*. Verbatim, this is how the poem will appear in my first book once I return home from the war. It's the quickest poem I've ever composed. I fold it up, place it in a Ziploc bag, and tuck it into the left front breast pocket of my DCU (desert combat uniform) top. I will carry it here—equal parts talisman and taunt—the rest of the time I am in-country. And I will often wonder who might find this poem if I am killed in combat. What would they think while opening the pleated zipper of the plastic bag, while unfolding the worn page, while reading the strange music in their hands?

1992. Fresno.

Backpack slung over my shoulder, hair halfway down my back and a scuba diver hanging by a silver hook from my earlobe, I'm walking across the campus at Fresno State. I'm a lathe operator (officially a machinist's assistant) at a small local company located in a rougher part of town. But tonight I'm simply walking on the grass under the street lamps and eucalyptus trees between buildings. I can hear the sprinkler heads in the distance, their hammered bursts of water traversing the grass. And although I don't remember where I picked up the poem (it was most likely given to me by the late Andrés Montoya, poet and author of *The Ice Worker Sings*), I have a photocopy of a poem by Phil Levine in my hands. And I don't fully realize that this moment, which seems mundane and innocuous on its surface, will affect my life profoundly for decades to come. This poem will influence my thoughts about what is possible in poetry and what is possible in language.

I begin with the title: "They Feed They Lion." Fresno disappears. The veiled membrane that separates worlds opens and the landscape of the poem stretches out before me. The grass turns to asphalt and concrete. And in the instant I read "out of the acids of rage, the candor of tar," I'm hooked. Here is a language that transports me and roots me solidly to the earth below. To be honest, I don't know what the hell is happening in the poem. And yet, it sings to the working-class rage I've inherited, it sings to the rage I've been steadily perfecting, hour by hour, in my life. It speaks to the nerves and blood and muscle I live in. It's a language I recognize immediately and yet have never heard before.

I've heard that Levine teaches at the college, and so I decide to take one of his classes to see what he is all about. I've taken several excellent poetry courses by this time in my life, and so I'm shocked by what I see on the first day of class. It's full. Every seat taken. In fact, people line the walls around the room, hoping to get a seat in the class. I've never seen anything like it. I haven't registered for the class. I'm not on the waiting list. Every poetry class I'd taken previously had always had at least one empty seat available for a poet wandering in from the street. More than once, I'd just walked in and signed up for class on the first day.

Midway through his introductory remarks (and before he asks everyone not registered or on the waiting list to leave), Levine excuses himself to grab some paperwork from his office. He looks around for a trash can and then, not finding one, he sets an empty tumbler on a desk as he steps out. I witness an odd thing at this point: I overhear a woman sitting near the tumbler say, under her breath, "That's Phil Levine's cup!" and she quickly grabs it and stows it away in her backpack. I laugh to myself as I stand against the wall, thinking, "Who the hell *is* this guy?"

At the end of the class, Levine is swamped by students trying to add it, checking to see whether he'll let them audit or simply sit in, as well as a couple of fans who want him to sign the books they've brought along. I'm incredibly shy at this point in my life, but I am also determined. In a very uncharacteristic moment for me, I approach him as he tries valiantly to leave the room. It's a moment I'll remember for years to come. The dingy fluorescent lights overhead. The square particleboards surrounding the lights in their plastic housings. The chalkboard behind him resolute in its darkened silence—its disquiet placed in question by a lone line of chalk running diagonally from right to left. And as other students linger in the hallway beyond the door, I say, "Mr. Levine, I don't care about grades and all of that bullshit. I just want to study with you."

Levine tilts his head back slightly, as if to see me from a different angle, weighing the person in front of him, I think, or so it seems. "Bring four or five poems by my office and we'll talk about it." And I do. A few days later, I'm sitting in an uncomfortable chair in what seems like the smallest office on campus, the many books on his shelves staring at me with their spines illuminated by light. My miserable poems are in his hands. Time slows to a held breath as he leafs through them.

He turns the papers over, resting them on his knee, and asks, "Who are you reading?" Nobody has ever asked me this before. I mention that I've been reading every book in the library by Pattiann Rogers that I could find this week and I notice a reaction on his face, but can't gauge what it means. I mention Octavio Paz. I name a string of writers whose work I've read recently and I tell him that I read anything that intrigues me—from medical textbooks covering advances in the surgical theater to the structural aspects of molecules to the mystical drug practices of the Yanomamö in South America.

In years to come, I'll realize how busy Levine must have been at this time in his life. I'll also recognize how he'd seen a long line of men and women like me. Hard-working people. Busted-up and broken people. People who knew that, if they weren't already, they just might live long enough to be busted-up and broken somewhere farther on down the road. And I'll realize that Levine must have recognized in me the deep and human need to create a space for the imagination. Levine understood the need to give voice to the San Joaquin Valley itself, the hard light it cast down in summer, the erasure of the world in the tule fog of January, the quiet beauty in the stoic people I loved. I think it is this—and not my rough poems he holds in his hands—that makes him create an independent study class for a small group of students, including me.

There are five of us in the class, and we meet once a week during Levine's last semester at Fresno State. We sit across from him along one edge of a long rectangular desk while he talks mostly about Keats and Lorca and Machado and Berryman and Crane. In his voice, I hear the tone of a man who speaks of these writers as if they are his close and lifelong friends. And, of course, that's exactly what they are. He's setting the bar. He's sharing his love for the art. The class itself follows a standard workshop model—poets read their work aloud, a pause is given for the poem to finish its time in the air, and then Levine regularly launches into his thoughts on the work itself, often threading the conversation out into the works of the greats who have come before us.

When I read my very first poem for the workshop (a poem set on a Venice Beach sidewalk; a poem about enjoying the human parade), Levine exhales a deep breath, turns the poem over and sets it firmly on the desk before him, saying to another student, "Byron, read your poem."

"Why don't you want to talk about my poem?" I ask him.

"You want me to talk about your poem?"

176

"Yeah. I want to know why you don't want to talk about my poem."

Levine is sizing me up. And it's in this moment that I am given a great gift. It's a shitty poem and we all know it. Still, he wants to make sure I really want what I'm asking for—the hard truth. I want him to skip the varnish most of us offer one another and tell me what he really thinks. And he does. He spends what feels like a good half an hour ripping the poem from one end to the other. It blows my hair back. It is exactly what I want, though it's difficult to hear.

We live such short lives. We don't have time for wisdom and knowledge to be doled out by the spoonful, year by slowly passing year. That's how I feel in the moment Levine rips into my poem and that's how I'll feel in years to come. No matter how hard it is to hear that I need to scrap nearly everything I'm doing, that my entire approach to the page is off the mark, that I need a serious god-damned kick in the ass as a poet—this is exactly why I approached Levine in the first place. He doesn't compliment my rhetorical flourishes, my pyrotechnics, my grand gestures in verse. He points to Machado. He points to Keats. He points to the poet I could be, perhaps, if I give it everything I have, and then some. If I give it my life.

For several years after the publication of my first book, I told people the story of how I wrote the title poem ("Here, Bullet") while listening to Queens of the Stone Age. But I was wrong. Although I wasn't aware of it at the time, I wasn't really listening to the music playing through those headphones. In fact, as I wrote the lines in my notebook and spoke the words under my breath, my ear traveled years back to the night I walked across the campus at Fresno State, reading "They Feed They Lion," while the sprinkler heads shifted from left to right, over and over.

It's so obvious when I read the first stanza of each poem aloud. It's so clear to me now. When I folded the poem I'd written and carried it through a year's combat duty in Iraq, there was nothing strange about it at all. I'd been carrying poetry inside of me for years. I'd carried Phil Levine's "They Feed They Lion" until the music rooted itself inside of me. And when I needed it most, when it was crucial, I was able to lean on that music so that I might bring my own words into the world.

A Walk with Philip Levine

ROBERT WRIGLEY

My first thought, on being invited to contribute to a collection of essays in celebration of Philip Levine, was a kind of delighted surprise. Delighted because there's no poet alive I'd rather celebrate, and surprised because I was never one of Phil's students. Not formally. I was never matriculated and enrolled at any institution or writers conference at which he taught. I was never in a classroom he was in charge of. He has never once sat down with me and showed me what's wrong or right or possible about a poem of mine.

I met Phil in the summer of 1988, at Bread Loaf Writers' Conference. I was a fellow; he was . . . well, he was Philip Levine. I'd published my second book about a year and a half earlier. I was thirty-seven; he was sixty, the age I am now. It was the year he published *A Walk with Tom Jefferson*. I'd heard him read the title poem at the AWP Conference and Bookfair, earlier that spring, in San Francisco. I heard him read it again at Bread Loaf. And the next winter, 1989, I drove eighty-five miles through shitty winter weather, to Gonzaga University in Spokane, and heard him read it yet again. It's been twenty-three years since I heard him read that poem, though I've read it many times since. To myself, of course, but also three or four times to classes. The whole thing. Just listen, I tell them. Sometimes I tell them about what it was like, hearing Phil read the poem that first time, in San Francisco. It was a huge hall, hundreds of people. Gerald Stern read, too. Stern was wonderful. But Levine read a poem that was, and is, transcendent. And I've never gotten over that reading, really. And I've never gotten over the poem.

What I mean to say is that Phil Levine, though he's never been my teacher, has been teaching me for a long time, teaching me what might be possible in this art of ours. "Tom Jefferson" is about a Levine-like speaker and about a black man in Detroit with the same name (sort of) as the republic's third president and principal national architect. It's about Detroit, about the riots of 1967; it's about capitalism, an economic system with the ideology of a cancer cell. It's about the United States of America and work and courage and outrage and heroic being. "It's Biblical," a repeated phrase from the poem, has come to be a kind of mantra of mine. Very often I say it at bleak political moments (as I did last night, in response to the latest lunatic assertion from Rick Santorum on the radio); the saying of it allows me to continue, to keep on, as Tom Jefferson kept on.

I bought my first book by Philip Levine in October 1975. I was in between my first and second years in graduate school at the University of Montana. Dick Hugo had come in to workshop that week, told us to quiet down and listen up. Then he read "They Feed They Lion." I wasn't quite sure what I'd heard when Dick finished reading. Which is to say, I'd never heard anything like it. Relentless and rhythmical and immensely powerful. I remember Dick looked around the seminar table at us, lit a cigarette, slid his glasses up on his forehead, and said: "Jesus Christ, people. That's a poem. That is a hell of a poem."

The book I bought later that day was *Red Dust*. I also ordered *They Feed They Lion* and *1933*, and I've been buying Phil's books ever since. According to Randall Jarrell's formulation, a good poet is someone who, "after a lifetime of standing out in thunderstorms, [has] managed to be struck by lightning five or six times," and that a great poet is someone who's struck "a dozen or two-dozen times." Most people who've read all or most of the body of Philip Levine's work already know he's a great poet. Get three or four such people in a room making up the list of such lightning strike poems, and the process gets out of hand in a hurry. My own list is ridiculously long.

But something about these two poems—"They Feed They Lion" and "A Walk with Tom Jefferson"—will not let me go. Or else they continue to illuminate a way—or several ways—to see and to say. They also insist, quite often, upon a measure of genuine social and political engagement that is daunting. I like to teach "They Feed They Lion" strictly as a sonic demonstration, as one of the most metrically intricate and incantatory passages of writing in the American canon, from the more-or-less syncopated iambic opening line, to the symmetrical spondees of line two, to the lunging anapests of line three. But it's not regular metrical construction; it's powerful rhythm in the service of powerful rhetoric—prophetic, elegiac, and soaring.

It's that voice, which is Phil Levine's at his most intense and impassioned through all his books, that has taught me and that has made me a student of his poems for nearly four decades now. I can attribute some of my poems directly to my reading of, my disassembly and examination of, Phil's poems. They don't sound like his poems; they couldn't. I couldn't make them that way. But the body of his work is my example, and by that example Philip Levine has been my mentor.

I've spent a few nights with Phil and Franny over the years: on a couple of visits to Fresno, where I slept in a bedroom up front in the house and lay awake for hours, looking through the photo albums stacked on the shelf of the nightstand by the bed; once in their apartment near the New York University campus, before they moved to Brooklyn. Phil introduced me at a reading one night in Fresno by pointing out that every time I'd been invited to Fresno, I'd won some sort of prize or fellowship (surely I'm due for another invitation). Another time, before we left for my reading, Phil had to have his son come over and program the VCR to record that night's episode of *The Sopranos*. Phil assured me that if the recording couldn't be done, he'd have to miss the reading. I'm pretty sure he was serious.

On the visit to New York, Phil and I took a long afternoon walk around the Village, Little Italy, Soho, and Chinatown. We talked about poems, teaching, the city, Fresno, Lorca, travel, and all sorts of other things. He and Franny and I went out to dinner at an Italian place in the Village that night. It was a lovely autumnal evening in New York, and I remember thinking about the great old Vernon Duke song "Autumn in New York" as we walked back to their apartment. It was a great moment for me, just walking across the city with Phil and Franny. I felt blessed by them, as I had been by Phil's poems.

But that other walk. In "A Walk with Tom Jefferson," the speaker takes his leave from Tom, who

locks the knee-high gate
of his fence that could
hold back no one

and the gaze of the speaker and the poem turn toward "the earth." We've
spent four hundred lines or so in the seemingly bombed-out, most assur-
edly burned, gutted, and despoiled wasteland of what had once been real and
vital neighborhoods of Detroit. Now we're moving back into the factories and
foundries so familiar in Phil's work, but we're also moving in the direction
of the earth, which has always underlain Detroit, which has given up the ore
that becomes the iron and steel of manufacture, which has offered up its

Beets the size of fists
by the thousands, cabbages
as big as brains
year after year, whole cribs
of peppers, great lakes
of sweet corn tumbling
by the trailer load.

In return, "whatever / we had it took," and that "took" in this instance is
beautifully ambiguous, managing to mean both accept and seize.

What *is* "A Walk with Tom Jefferson" after? Sure, it's an indictment of
capitalism and its relentless devouring of human capital, or human fuel.
It's an indictment of racism, of course. Yes, there's an immense rage in the
poem, but there are two other significant emotional and intellectual qualities
equal to that rage. One, of course, is sadness; the burned cityscape the poet
describes is the city of his birth. But there is also—and I don't think there's
any other word for this—celebration—for the resilience of Tom Jefferson
himself, which is also the resilience of the republic of which Philip Levine
became the poet laureate. And for the wonderful nature of the human animal
itself, which at its best not only abides, but finds a way to sing.

And the singing is the poem. Listen to the tone of the poem's conclusion,
from when the hayseed, factory co-worker asks, "what was we making." Yes,
there's humor in the speaker's admitted misunderstanding at first, but the
"kid just up / from West Virginia" corrects him, "gently":

what was
we making out of
this here metal?

I love how, based on the name of the place—

> "Chevrolet
> Gear & Axle"
> right on the checks they paid
> us with

—the speaker can still only "half-believe" that's what they made with their machines.

It seems to me that those who "half-believe" might be the truest patriots among us. True believers, it seems, run for office and entirely too often get elected. The half-believers draw from the "earth tomatoes," as Tom Jefferson says, that "remind you what tomatoes / taste like." Or else, in the case of Philip Levine, they make of the raw materials of the earth and the languages of its inhabitants, of the half-belief in tomorrow and glory and the ruins of the past, a way of seeing what we are. And I half-believe, thanks to Phil Levine, that we are beautiful nevertheless.

Back in the late eighties, I once wrote out, by hand, the entirety of "A Walk with Tom Jefferson." It was something I did with poems I'd become obsessed with. I think I wanted a way inside the poem's structure; I wanted to understand its motions and its machinery. I've studied the poem, and through it I have learned from its author a great deal about poetry and possibilities, and about this life we all live. There may not be any poems written during the years of my life that I would rather have written than "A Walk with Tom Jefferson." Knowing what I know, I would say, among many other things, that I can half-believe it, too.

Contributors

AARON BELZ is the author of *Plausible Worlds* (Observable, 2005), *The Bird Hoverer* (BlazeVOX, 2007), and *Lovely, Raspberry* (Persea, 2010). He lives in Hillsborough, North Carolina.

CIARAN BERRY's first collection, *The Sphere of Birds*, was published in North America by Southern Illinois University Press in 2008. His work has appeared in the *Best American Poetry*, *Pushcart*, and *Best New Poets* anthologies as well as a number of journals, including *AGNI*, *Crazyhorse*, *Ploughshares*, *The Missouri Review*, and *The Threepenny Review*.

PAULA BOHINCE is the author of two poetry collections, both from Sarabande: *The Children* (2012) and *Incident at the Edge of Bayonet Woods* (2008). Her poems have appeared in *The New Yorker*, *Poetry*, *The Times Literary Supplement*, *Poetry London*, and *The Yale Review*. She has received fellowships from the National Endowment for the Arts, the Amy Clampitt Trust, and the Bread Loaf Writers' Conference, as well as the "Discovery"/*The Nation* Award and the Amy Lowell Poetry Travelling Scholarship. She lives in Pennsylvania.

SHANE BOOK's first collection, *Ceiling of Sticks*, won the 2009 Prairie Schooner Book Prize, the 2012 Great Lakes Colleges Association New Writers Award, and was a 2011 Poetry Society of America "New American Poet" Selection. He is a graduate of New York University and the Iowa Writers' Workshop and was a Stegner Fellow at Stanford University. His work has appeared in numerous anthologies and magazines in the United States, the United Kingdom, and

Canada—and on film. His honors include a *New York Times* Fellowship in Poetry, fellowships to the Flaherty Film Seminar and Telluride Film Festival, an Academy of American Poets Prize, and a National Magazine Award.

B. H. BOSTON received his BA in English from California State University, Fresno, and his MFA from the Writing Program at the University of California–Irvine. His work has appeared in numerous magazines, including *Crazyhorse, Black Warrior Review, Western Humanities Review, Ploughshares,* and *Blackbird,* as well as in various anthologies. His most recent collection of poems, *By All Lights,* was published by Tebot Bach Press. Boston is Co–Poetry Editor for *Poetry International* at San Diego State University and curator of the Master Author Residency Program at La Jolla Country Day School in La Jolla.

XOCHIQUETZAL CANDELARIA is the author of *Empire,* published by the University of Arizona Press. Her work has appeared in *The Nation, The New England Review, Gulf Coast, The Seneca Review,* and other literary journals. She holds an MFA degree from New York University and has received multiple fellowships, including from the Bread Loaf Writers' Conference and the National Endowment for the Arts. She teaches at San Francisco City College.

COLIN CHENEY's debut collection of poems, *Here Be Monsters* (University of Georgia, 2010), was selected for the National Poetry Series. His poems have appeared in *American Poetry Review, Guernica, Poetry, Ploughshares, Kenyon Review, Crazyhorse,* and *Gulf Coast.* He has received a Ruth Lilly Poetry Fellowship and a Pushcart Prize. He is a founding editor of *Tongue: A Journal of Writing & Art.* He lives in Bangkok with his wife and daughter.

MICHAEL CLIFTON was born in Reedley, California, in 1949 and grew up on various army bases around the world before his family settled in Fresno in 1960. He attended California State University, Fresno, where he received both a BA and an MA in English before getting a PhD in American Literature at Indiana University, Bloomington. He teaches at California State University, Fresno, and has poems included in *Down at the Santa Fe Depot: Twenty Fresno Poets* and *How Much Earth: The Fresno Poets. Whatever Lasts in Winter,* published by Tebot Bach in 2004, is his first book-length publication.

MICHAEL COLLIER's most recent collection of poems is *An Individual History* (W. W. Norton, 2012). He teaches in the creative writing program at the University of Maryland and is the director of the Bread Loaf Writers' Conference.

NICOLE COOLEY grew up in New Orleans and is the author most recently of two collections of poems, *Breach* (LSU Press, 2010) and *Milk Dress* (Alice James Books, 2010). She has also published two other books of poems and a novel. She directs the new MFA Program in Creative Writing and Literary Translation at Queens College–City University of New York where she is a professor of English. She lives outside of New York City with her husband and two daughters.

KATE DANIELS is the author of four volumes of poetry, including *A Walk in Victoria's Secret*, her most recent. She has written frequently on Philip Levine's poetry and was the organizer of a celebration of his seventy-fifth birthday at Vanderbilt University in the spring of 2003. Currently, she is professor of English and director of creative writing at Vanderbilt University.

BLAS MANUEL DE LUNA was born in Tijuana, Mexico, and raised in Madera, California. He received an MA in English from California State University, Fresno, and an MFA from the University of Washington, where he was the first Klepser Fellow. In 1998, he was an Artist Trust/Washington States Art Commission Literature Fellow. During the 2000–2001 academic year, he was the Jay C. and Ruth Halls Poetry Fellow at the University of Wisconsin, Madison. His poetry collection, *Bent to the Earth*, published by Carnegie Mellon University Press, was a finalist for the 2006 National Book Critics Circle Award in Poetry.

KATHY FAGAN is the author of four collections of poems, most recently *Lip*. Work from a fifth collection, *Sycamore* (in progress), appeared in *The Laurel Review, theawl.com, FIELD, Cimarron Review*, and *Ocean State Review*. Fagan holds fellowships from the National Endowment for the Arts, the Ingram Merrill Foundation, and the Ohio Arts Council. She teaches at Ohio State, where she coedits the OSU Press/*The Journal* Award Series in Poetry.

ANDREW FELD is the author of *Citizen* (HarperCollins, 2004), a 2003 National Poetry Series selection, and *Raptor* (University of Chicago Press, 2012). His honors include the "Discovery"/*The Nation* Award, two Pushcart Prizes, and work in the Best American Poetry series. He is an associate professor at the University of Washington and editor-in-chief of *The Seattle Review*.

NICK FLYNN's most recent book is *The Captain Asks for a Show of Hands*, a collection of poems linked to his memoir *The Ticking Is the Bomb*. His previous memoir, *Another Bullshit Night in Suck City*, won the PEN/Martha Albrand Award and was adapted into the film *Being Flynn*, released in 2012 (Focus Features). He is also the author of two other books of poetry, *Some Ether* and *Blind Huber*. Each spring he teaches in the creative writing program at the University of Houston and then spends the rest of the year in (or near) Brooklyn.

EDWARD HIRSCH has published eight books of poems, including *The Living Fire: New and Selected Poems* (2010), and four books of prose, among them *How to Read a Poem and Fall in Love with Poetry* (1999), a national best seller. He has taught at Wayne State University and the University of Houston and now serves as president of the John Simon Guggenheim Memorial Foundation.

SANDRA HOBEN's poetry has appeared in *Alaska Quarterly Review, Antioch Review, Ironwood, Naugatuck River Review, Partisan Review, Quarterly West, Raleigh Review, Speechless: Online Poetry Magazine, Three Rivers Poetry Journal*, and *Western Humanities Review* as well as in the anthologies *Claiming the Spirit Within: A Sourcebook of Women's Poetry, Tangled Vines: A Collection of Mother & Daughter Poems, How Much Earth: The Fresno Poets, Beside the Sleeping Maiden, Bear Flag Republic: Prose Poems and Poetics from California*, and *Aspects of Robinson: Homage to Weldon Kees*. Her letterpress chapbook *Snow Flowers* was published by Westigan Press, and she has a forthcoming volume from Ash Tree Poetry Series.

ISHION HUTCHINSON was born in Port Antonio, Jamaica. He is a recipient of the Academy of American Poets' Larry Levis Memorial Prize and the 2011 PEN/Joyce Osterweil Award for Poetry for his first collection, *Far District: Poems* (Peepal Tree Press, 2010). He is currently a Pirogue Fellow and an assistant professor of English at Cornell University.

LAWSON FUSAO INADA is a third-generation Japanese American from Fresno, California. As a child during World War II, he was imprisoned in California, Arkansas, and Colorado. A graduate of Fresno State University and the University of Oregon, he is professor emeritus at Southern Oregon University. His books of poetry are *Before the War, Legends from Camp*, and *Drawing the Line*. He is the editor of *Only What We Could Carry: The Japanese American Internment Experience*. His honors include an Oregon Book Award, an American Book Award, and fellowships from the National Endowment for the Arts and the Guggenheim Foundation. He has served as Oregon Poet Laureate.

DORIANNE LAUX's first book, *Awake*, was published by BOA Editions in 1990 with an introduction by Philip Levine. Her most recent collection, *The Book of Men* (W. W. Norton, 2011), is dedicated to Philip Levine. Laux teaches poetry in the MFA program at North Carolina State University and is a founding faculty member at Pacific University's low-residency Master of Fine Arts in Writing Program.

JOSEPH O. LEGASPI is the author of *Imago* (CavanKerry Press). Recent poems appeared in *From the Fishouse, jubilat, World Literature Today, The Spoon River Poetry Review, Smartish Pace, PEN International,* and *The Normal School*. A resident of Queens, New York, he cofounded Kundiman, a nonprofit organization serving Asian American poets.

MARI L'ESPERANCE was born in Kobe, Japan, to a Japanese mother and a French Canadian–American father. Her poetry collection *The Darkened Temple* (University of Nebraska Press) was awarded a Prairie Schooner Book Prize. An earlier collection, *Begin Here*, was awarded a Sarasota Poetry Theatre Press Chapbook Prize. L'Esperance holds graduate degrees in creative writing from New York University and in counseling psychology from John F. Kennedy University in Northern California. The recipient of awards from *The New York Times*, New York University, Hedgebrook, and Dorland Mountain Arts Colony, L'Esperance lives in the Los Angeles area.

MARK LEVINE has written three books of poems, most recently *The Wilds*, and a book of nonfiction, as well as articles for publications including *The New Yorker, Outside,* and *The New York Times Magazine*. Since 1999 he has taught poetry at the Iowa Writers' Workshop.

LARRY LEVIS (1946–1996) published five poetry collections during his life, including *The Widening Spell of the Leaves* and *Winter Stars*. Posthumously, two books of poetry, *Elegy* and *The Selected Levis: Poems 1972–1992*, have been published, as well as a collection of essays, interviews, and reviews, *The Gazer Within*. Levis won many awards, including the Lamont Poetry Prize; was selected for the National Poetry Series; and received fellowships from the National Endowment for the Arts, the Guggenheim Foundation, and the Fulbright Program. He taught at Virginia Commonwealth University.

ADA LIMÓN is the author of three books of poetry including, most recently, *Sharks in the Rivers*. Her work has appeared in numerous magazines, including *The New Yorker* and *Harvard Review*. She is currently finishing her first novel, a book of essays, and a new collection of poems. She works as a writer and lives in both Kentucky and California.

ELLINE LIPKIN is currently a research scholar with the Center for the Study of Women at the University of California, Los Angeles. She received her MFA in poetry from Columbia University and her PhD in literature/creative writing from the University of Houston. Her book *The Errant Thread* was chosen by Eavan Boland for the Kore Press First Book Award and published in 2006. Her nonfiction book, *Girls' Studies*, explores the gendering of girls in contemporary America and was published by Seal Press in 2009.

JANE MEAD is the author of three full-length collections of poetry and a recipient of grants and awards from the Guggenheim, Whiting, and Lannan foundations. For many years poet-in-residence at Wake Forest University, she now teaches in the low-residency MFA program at Drew University and farms in Northern California.

DANTE MICHEAUX is the author of *Amorous Shepherd* (Sheep Meadow Press, 2010). His poems and translations have appeared in *The American Poetry Review, Bloom, Callaloo, Gathering Ground*, and *Rattapallax*—among other journals and anthologies. He has been short-listed for the Benjamin Zephaniah Poetry Prize and the Bridport Prize. Micheaux's honors include a prize in poetry from the Vera List Center for Art and Politics, the Oscar Wilde Award, and fellowships from the Cave Canem Foundation and *The New York Times* Foundation. He lives in London and New York City.

TOMÁS Q. MORÍN is the author of *A Larger Country*, winner of the *American Poetry Review*/Honickman First Book Prize. He is the recipient of scholarships from the Fine Arts Work Center, the New York State Summer Writers Institute, and the Bread Loaf Writers' Conference. His poems have appeared in *New England Review, Narrative, Boulevard, Threepenny Review, Slate*, and *American Poetry Review*.

MALENA MÖRLING is the author of two books of poetry, *Ocean Avenue* and *Astoria*. She has translated several Swedish poets and is editing the anthology *Swedish Writers on Writing*. She is an associate professor at the University of North Carolina, Wilmington; core faculty in the low-residency MFA program at New England College; and a research associate at the School for Advanced

Research on the Human Experience in Santa Fe, New Mexico. She received a Guggenheim Fellowship in 2007 and a Lannan Foundation Literary Fellowship in 2010.

JOHN MURILLO is the author of the poetry collection *Up Jump the Boogie* (Cypher 2010) and a finalist for both the 2011 Kate Tufts Discovery Award and the PEN Open Book Award. His other honors include a Pushcart Prize, two Larry Neal Writers' Awards, and fellowships from the Cave Canem Foundation, *The New York Times*, the Wisconsin Institute of Creative Writing, Bread Loaf Writers' Conference, and the Fine Arts Work Center in Provincetown, Massachusetts. Currently, he serves on the creative writing faculty at New York University.

DANIEL NESTER is the author of *How to Be Inappropriate*, a collection of humorous nonfiction; *God Save My Queen: A Tribute* and *God Save My Queen II: The Show Must Go On*, collections on his obsession with the rock band Queen; and *The History of My World Tonight*, a collection of poems. He is an associate professor of English at the College of Saint Rose in Albany, New York.

SHARON OLDS is the author of nine books of poetry. *The Dead and the Living* received the National Book Critics Circle Award; *The Unswept Room* was a finalist for the National Book Award and the National Book Critics Circle Award; and *One Secret Thing* was a finalist for the Forward Prize. She teaches at New York University's graduate Creative Writing Program, where she has been involved with NYU's outreach workshops. The Goldwater Hospital workshop is in its twenty-seventh year, and the newest workshop is for veterans of the wars in Iraq and Afghanistan. Her latest collection of poetry, *Stag's Leap*, was published in 2012. She lives in New York City and New Hampshire.

JANUARY GILL O'NEIL is the author of *Underlife* (CavanKerry Press, 2009) and a forthcoming collection, *Misery Islands* (CavanKerry Press). She is the executive director of the Massachusetts Poetry Festival and an assistant professor of English at Salem State University.

GREG PAPE's books include *Border Crossings, Black Branches, Storm Pattern, Sunflower Facing the Sun, American Flamingo*, and *Animal Time*. He has received the "Discovery"/*The Nation* Award, two National Endowment for the Arts Fellowships, the Pushcart Prize, the Edwin Ford Piper Prize, the Crab Orchard Open Competition Award, and the Richard Hugo Memorial Poetry

Award. He teaches at the University of Montana and in the brief-residency MFA program at Spalding University. He served as Montana Poet Laureate during 2007–2009.

KATHLEEN PEIRCE is the author of four books of poems. She teaches poetry in the MFA program at Texas State University. Her work has been awarded the AWP Donald Hall Prize for Poetry, the Iowa Poetry Prize, and the William Carlos Williams Award and supported by fellowships from the Whiting Foundation, the National Endowment for the Arts, and the Guggenheim Foundation.

SAM PEREIRA's books include *The Marriage of the Portuguese* (L'Epervier Press, 1978), *Brittle Water* (Abattoir Editions/Penumbra Press, 1987), and *A Cafe in Boca* (Tebot Bach, 2007). An expanded edition of the first book was published in 2012 by Tagus Press at the University of Massachusetts, Dartmouth. His latest book is *Dusting on Sunday*. He lives and teaches in California.

JEFFREY SKINNER's prose book *The 6.5 Practices of Moderately Successful Poets* (Sarabande Books) appeared in April 2012. Also a photographer, he mounted a recent show of his work at Pyro Gallery in Louisville, Kentucky. His latest book of poems, *Glaciology*, was a winner in the 2012 Crab Orchard Series in Poetry Open Competition Awards and will be published by Southern Illinois University Press in 2013. Jeffrey expects this book to be moderately successful.

TOM SLEIGH is the author of eight books of poetry, including *Army Cats* and *Space Walk*, which won the 2008 Kingsley Tufts Poetry Award. He has received the Shelley Memorial Award from the Poetry Society of America, a fellowship from the American Academy in Berlin, the John Updike Award, and an Academy Award from the American Academy of Arts and Letters, an Individual Writer's Award from the Lila Wallace–Reader's Digest Fund, a Guggenheim Foundation grant, and two National Endowment for the Arts grants, among many others. He teaches in the MFA Program at Hunter College and lives in Brooklyn.

DAVID ST. JOHN is the author of ten collections of poetry (including *Study for the World's Body*, nominated for the National Book Award in Poetry), most recently *The Auroras*, and a volume of essays, interviews, and reviews titled *Where the Angels Come toward Us*. He is also the coeditor, with Cole Swensen, of *American Hybrid: A Norton Anthology of New Poetry*. He has been honored with fellowships from the National Endowment for the Arts and the John Simon Guggenheim Memorial Foundation and has received both the Rome Prize Fellowship and an Award in Literature from the American Academy and Institute of Arts and Letters.

BRIAN TURNER is the author of *Here, Bullet* and *Phantom Noise* (both from Alice James Books). He has received a USA Hillcrest Fellowship in Literature, a Literature Fellowship in Poetry from the National Endowment for the Arts, the Amy Lowell Poetry Travelling Scholarship, a Japan–United States Friendship Commission grant, the Poets' Prize, and a Lannan Foundation Fellowship. His work has appeared on National Public Radio, the BBC, *PBS NewsHour*, and *Weekend America*, among others. He is the director of the low-residency MFA program at Sierra Nevada College.

ROBERT WRIGLEY teaches in the MFA program at the University of Idaho. A former Guggenheim and two-time National Endowment for the Arts Fellow, his books include *Beautiful Country* (Penguin, 2010); *Lives of the Animals* (Penguin, 2003), winner of the Poets' Prize; and *Reign of Snakes* (Penguin, 1999), winner of the Kingsley Tufts Poetry Award. *Anatomy of Melancholy & Other Poems* is forthcoming (from Penguin) in 2013. He once drove Phil Levine from Lewiston, Idaho, to Missoula, Montana, up the Lochsa River, and over Lolo Pass, listening to Archie Shepp and Horace Parlan all the way. Robert Johnson (not that one) was in the back seat.